PENGUIN PASSNOTES

Mathematics

Ian Dawbarn was educated at York University where he took a B.A. (Hons) and at Oxford University where he received an M.Sc. He has subsequently taught in a number of schools in Oxford and is now Tutor in Mathematics at Davies's College, London. He has written several study guides in the Penguin Passnotes series and is an examiner for a major GCE examining board.

PENGUIN PASSNOTES

Mathematics

IAN DAWBARN

ADVISORY EDITOR: STEPHEN COOTE, M.A., PH.D.

PENGUIN BOOKS

Penguin Books Ltd, Harmondsworth, Middlesex, England
Viking Penguin Inc., 40 West 23rd Street, New York, New York 10010, U.S.A.
Penguin Books Australia Ltd, Ringwood, Victoria, Australia
Penguin Books Canada Limited, 2801 John Street, Markham, Ontario, Canada L3R 1B4
Penguin Books (N.Z.) Ltd, 182–190 Wairau Road, Auckland 10, New Zealand

First published 1984
Reprinted 1985, 1986

Filmset in Monophoto Times Roman by
Northumberland Press Ltd, Gateshead, Tyne and Wear
Made and printed in Great Britain by
Richard Clay (The Chaucer Press) Ltd, Bungay, Suffolk

*The publishers are grateful to the following Examination Boards
for permission to reproduce questions from examination papers used
in individual titles in the Passnotes series:*

*Associated Examining Board, University of Cambridge Local Examinations Syndicate,
Joint Matriculation Board, University of London School Examinations Department,
Oxford and Cambridge Schools Examination Board, University of Oxford Delegacy of
Local Examinations.*

*The Examination Boards accept no responsibility whatsoever for the accuracy or
method of working in any suggested answers given as models.*

Contents

Introduction

Success in mathematics depends on understanding the basic principles thoroughly, and on setting out your answers to problems in a clear, logical and *accurate* way. This book is designed to help in both of these areas.

The 'O' level mathematics syllabuses of all the major examining boards are represented. Each section covers the essential theory for understanding a topic, and a large number of worked examination questions. In most cases, the examples are set out as model answers. They show how much detail and explanation are required in your answer.

An examination answer must be clear and accurate. When working through the examples, make sure that you understand all of the steps involved. To help you, comments to guide you through the working are listed on the right of the model answers. Accuracy is particularly important for numerical work. It is good practice to check all of your working at least once; it does not take long and is worthwhile in terms of marks.

Several multiple-choice questions are included. For these also, you should work through the problem completely, as though it were an ordinary question. An inspired guess is very seldom correct!

Although each section is self-contained, the book is best used as a whole. Page references are included throughout to help you find your way about the book.

A list of terms and definitions is included at the back, for easy reference while using the book, and also some general rules about using tables and calculators. All questions taken from Examination Boards are printed in italics for easy reference; worked examples which are not printed in italics are examination-*type* questions devised by the author.

Notation Used

$\{\dots\}$	the set of ... (elements listed in brackets)
$n(A)$	the number of elements in set A
$\{x : \dots\}$	the set of all x such that ...
$\in$	is an element of
$\notin$	is not an element of
ϕ	the empty set
ξ	the universal set
$\cup$	union
$\cap$	intersection
$\subset$	is a subset of
A'	the complement of the set A
PQ	operation Q followed by operation P
$\overrightarrow{AB}$	the vector from A to B
$f : A \to B$	function taking elements of set A to elements of B
$f : x \to y$	function taking x to y
$f(x)$	the result of doing f to x
f^{-1}	the inverse of the function f
fg	function g followed by function f
○———○	section (interval) of the number line without its end points
●———●	section of the number line with its end points
a	a vector
$p(A)$	probability of the event A
$<, \leqslant$	less than, less than or equal to
$>, \geqslant$	greater than, greater than or equal to
∞	infinity
*	number operation

Section 1: Numbers

Much of mathematics is about the use and properties of numbers. Understanding how to work with them is essential for most of the course. There are several different types of numbers: whole numbers, fractions and decimals.

0, 1, 2, 3, ... are the positive whole numbers, called the *natural numbers*. If the negative whole numbers are also included, the collection is called the *integers*, ..., −3, −2, −1, 0, 1, 2, 3, ... where the dots indicate that the list continues indefinitely in both directions.

You can imagine the integers as divisions on a *number line*.

$$-5 \quad -4 \quad -3 \quad -2 \quad -1 \quad 0 \quad 1 \quad 2 \quad 3 \quad 4 \quad 5$$

The numbers counting steps to the right are positive or + numbers, while those to the left are negative or − numbers. The positive numbers are written without a sign, but the + should be understood. Putting a − sign in front of a + number has the effect of 'flipping' it over the 0 mark:

$$-5 \quad -4 \quad -3 \quad -2 \quad -1 \quad 0 \quad 1 \quad 2 \quad 3 \quad 4 \quad 5$$

$-(+2) = -2$; in other words $-(+) = -$

Putting a − sign in front of a negative number flips it back on to the right-hand side of the line:

$$-5 \quad -4 \quad -3 \quad -2 \quad -1 \quad 0 \quad 1 \quad 2 \quad 3 \quad 4 \quad 5$$

$-(-2) = +2$; in other words $-(-) = +$

This would happen no matter what number you started with. The rules can be written without numbers as

$$-(+) = -, \; -(-) = +, \; +(-) = -, \; +(+) = +$$

and are used for combining signs together. You must remember them. The brackets are used to keep the signs separated to avoid misunderstanding. $- -2$ could easily be misread as -2. Brackets can be very useful for making things clearer, as you will see in later sections.

Combining Numbers

Numbers can be combined by adding and subtracting. Two numbers can be added in either order and the result is the same: $2 + 3$ and $3 + 2$ are both equal to 5. In subtraction the order *is* important, $3 - 2 = 1$, while $2 - 3 = -1$.

Examples 1. $-5 + 4 = +4 - 5$ swapping numbers around a $+$ has no effect

$\qquad\qquad\quad = -1$

$\qquad$ 2. $3 - 7 = -4$ Changing the order of two numbers

but $\qquad\qquad 7 - 3 = +4$ to be subtracted introduces an extra $-$ sign in front of the answer $-(-4) = +4$

It is easy to make a mistake while subtracting in your head, particularly when negative numbers are around. It often helps if you show the subtraction on a number line:

$2 - 3$ means start at 2 and move 3 steps to the left; the result is -1.

Multiplying
When multiplying numbers, multiply the signs separately.

Example $(-2) \times 3 = (-2) \times (+3)$ putting in the $+$ sign
$\qquad\qquad\qquad = (-)(+)(2 \times 3)$ splitting off the signs
$\qquad\qquad\qquad = (-)(6)$ using the rule $-(+) = -$
$\qquad\qquad\qquad = -6$

The rule is much the same for *division*, where the rules for combining the signs are the same as for multiplying.

Example $4 \div (-2) = +4 \div (-2)$
$\qquad\qquad\quad = (+)(-)(4 \div 2)$
$\qquad\qquad\quad = -2$ as $(+)(-) = -$

In this example, the 2 divides the 4 exactly, it is called a *factor* of 4. On the other hand, 3 is not a factor of 4, as it leaves a *remainder* of 1 when the 3 is divided out.

Fractions

Dividing one whole number by another gives a fraction. For example $4 \div 5$ is written as the fraction $\frac{4}{5}$. The bar in the middle stands for division. The fraction $\frac{4}{5}$ is not a whole number. You can find it on the number line by cutting a length into 5 equal pieces, and counting 4 of them:

$\frac{4}{5}$ is between 0 and 1.

Some fractions are also whole numbers: $\frac{4}{2} = 4 \div 2 = 2$. Conversely, any whole number can be written as a fraction by putting it over a 1. For example $5 = \frac{5}{1}$. The bottom number is called the *denominator* of the fraction, and the top is called the *numerator*.

Using these ideas, $\frac{4}{2} = 4 \div 2 = 2 = \frac{2}{1}$. The two fractions $\frac{4}{2}$ and $\frac{2}{1}$ are the same, and the second one can be obtained from the first by dividing out the factor 2 which is common to both top and bottom. This process of dividing out common factors can be used over and over again until the top and bottom of the fraction have no factors in common. The fraction is then said to be in its *lowest terms*. Whenever a fraction is the answer to a calculation you should write it in its lowest terms.

Example Write the fraction $\frac{20}{16}$ in its lowest terms.

Answer   4 is a common factor, so dividing it out from top and bottom leaves $\frac{5}{4}$.

When the numerator of the fraction is larger than the denominator, the fraction can be expressed as a *mixed number*. 4 divides into 5 once with a remainder of 1, so the fraction can be written as $1\frac{1}{4}$. The number of times the division can be done is the integer in front, and the fraction part is the remainder over the denominator.

A mixed number can also be written as a fraction, for example

$$2\frac{1}{3} = \frac{2 \times 3 + 1}{3} = \frac{7}{3}$$

Adding and subtracting fractions

When two fractions have the same denominator, they can be added or subtracted by dealing with the numerators only. For example

$$\frac{2}{3} + \frac{4}{3} = \frac{2+4}{3} \qquad \text{add the tops}$$

$$= \frac{6}{3}$$

$$= \frac{2}{1} \qquad \text{divide by common factor 3}$$

$$= 2 \qquad \text{leave the 1 out}$$

However, in most cases the denominators of the fractions will be different. They can be made to be the same by multiplying the fraction by suitable factors on the top and bottom.

Example *Write as a single fraction $\frac{1}{4} + \frac{3}{5}$ (AEB part)*

Answer   Multiplying by 5 in the first fraction, and by 4 in the second

$$\frac{5}{20} + \frac{12}{20} = \frac{5+12}{20}$$

the denominators are now the same, so the tops can be added; the answer is $\frac{17}{20}$.

Multiplying and dividing fractions

Multiplying is easier: just multiply the tops and bottoms separately.

Example Write as a single fraction $\frac{2}{3} \times \frac{4}{5}$

Answer $\dfrac{2 \times 4}{3 \times 5} = \dfrac{8}{15}$

When one of the numbers to be multiplied is a whole number, it should first be converted into a fraction by putting it over the denominator 1.

Example Write as a single fraction $2 \times \frac{4}{3}$

Answer $\dfrac{2}{1} \times \dfrac{4}{3} = \dfrac{2 \times 4}{1 \times 3} = \dfrac{8}{3}$

To divide by a fraction, turn it upside down and multiply it.

Example *Write as a single fraction* $\frac{1}{7} \div \frac{1}{5}$ (A E B part)

Answer   Turn the second fraction and change the $\div$ to $\times$

$$\frac{1}{7} \times \frac{5}{1} = \frac{1 \times 5}{7 \times 1}$$

$$= \frac{5}{7}$$

The result of turning a fraction upside down is its *reciprocal*. To find the reciprocal of a whole number, write it as a fraction first. The reciprocal of 2, which is $\frac{2}{1}$, is $\frac{1}{2}$. Notice that the reciprocal of $\frac{1}{2}$ is $\frac{2}{1}$ which is the same as 2.

Example
Work out $(2\frac{1}{3} - 1\frac{1}{5}) \div \frac{3}{4}$

Answer	**Comments**
$\left(2\frac{1}{3} - 1\frac{1}{5}\right) \div \frac{3}{4} = \left(\frac{7}{3} - \frac{6}{5}\right) \div \frac{3}{4}$	first change the mixed numbers into fractions
$= \left(\frac{35}{15} - \frac{18}{15}\right) \div \frac{3}{4}$	make the denominators in the brackets the same by multiplying by 3 and by 5
$= \left(\frac{35 - 18}{15}\right) \div \frac{3}{4}$	
$= \frac{17}{15} \div \frac{3}{4}$	subtract the tops
$= \frac{17}{15} \times \frac{4}{3}$	turn the second fraction
$= \frac{17 \times 4}{15 \times 3}$	multiply separately
$= \frac{68}{45}$	divide by common factor 3
$= 1\frac{23}{45}$	write as a mixed fraction

Always write out all the steps of a calculation like this, and check each line. Careless mistakes cost marks.

Decimal Numbers

A decimal number looks like 236·123, with a *decimal point*, ·, separating the digits. It represents the mixed number $236\frac{123}{1\,000}$. The number of zeros in the denominator of the fraction part is the same as the number of digits after the decimal point. The point is used to separate the whole number part from the fractional part.

Multiplying a decimal number by 10 moves the decimal point one place to the right. Dividing by 10 moves the point one place to the left.

$$236{\cdot}123 \times 10 = 2\,361{\cdot}23 \qquad 236{\cdot}123 \div 10 = 23.6123$$

Dividing or multiplying by 100 moves the point two places, by 1 000 moves it three places, and so on.

The decimal point should always have digits on both sides, filling in with zeros if necessary. So you should write 0·1 and not ·1, 2·0 and not 2·.

Fractions and mixed numbers can be written as decimals by dividing out by the denominator.

$$\frac{3}{5} = \frac{2 \times 3}{2 \times 5}$$

multiplying top and bottom does not change its value; division by

$$= \frac{6}{10}$$

10 is easier than division by 5, and since $10 = 5 \times 2$, the factor to use is 2)

$$= \frac{6{\cdot}0}{10}$$

putting in the decimal point

$$= 0{\cdot}6$$

moving the point one place to the left

The division was made easier by arranging for the denominator to be 10 by suitable multiplication. This is a good technique, but is not always possible. In other cases you could do the long division by hand or use a calculator or tables (see p. 222).

To convert a mixed number, split off the fraction part and write that as a decimal as above. Then add this decimal to the integer part. $\frac{1}{4} = 0{\cdot}25$ so that $1\frac{1}{4} = 1{\cdot}25$.

Some fractions cannot be written exactly as decimals, the fraction $\frac{1}{3}$ for example. Doing the long division gives the answer 0·3333 ..., where the list of 3s does not come to an end. This is called a *recurring decimal*. A decimal like this that has an unlimited number of digits after the point can only be written down to a certain number of *decimal places*. $\frac{1}{3} = 0·333$ to 3 decimal-place accuracy; to 6 decimal-place accuracy it is 0·333333. The number of decimal places is the number of digits after the decimal point.

Usually, in calculations and measurement, there is a limit to the accuracy that the numbers can have. The accuracy is often given by specifying the number of decimal places. A number given to 3 decimal-place accuracy means that it should be correct at least up to the *second* decimal place (the last digit may be rounded up).

The answers to numerical calculations usually have to be rounded off to a certain number of decimal places.

Examples 1·37156 to 2 decimal places is 1·37|156 (chopping off the last three digits) leaving the answer 1·37

1·37156 to 3 decimal places: 1·371|56, the first digit to be chopped off is 5, and in this case the preceding digit has to be *rounded up* to 2, giving the answer 1·372

The rounding up must be done whenever the first digit to be cut off is 5 or larger.

The level of accuracy can also be specified as the number of *significant figures*, starting from the first non-zero digit on the left.

Examples 2 317·56 to 3 significant figures is 231|7·56 where the digits 7·56 must be ignored; they are replaced by 0s. The answer is 2 310·0, or simply 2 310.

Give 0·01235 to 3 significant figures. Start counting from the 1, as all the other digits on the left are 0s. 0·0123|5. Again the rounding up comes into play, as the digit to be cut off is 5. The answer is 0·0124.

An examination question will almost always specify the accuracy to which the numbers should be expressed. Make sure that you follow these instructions. Giving the correct answer, but to the wrong accuracy, will lose you marks.

Adding and subtracting decimals

The decimal points should always be lined up one above the other

$$
\begin{array}{r}
23{\cdot}17 \\
+\ \ 1{\cdot}24 \\
\hline
24{\cdot}41
\end{array}
\qquad
\begin{array}{r}
51{\cdot}701 \\
-\ \ 2{\cdot}65 \\
\hline
49{\cdot}051
\end{array}
$$

Multiplying decimals

First multiply the numbers, ignoring the *decimal points*. The number of decimal places of the product is the sum of the decimal places of the separate numbers.

$$
\begin{array}{rl}
23{\cdot}1 & \text{1 decimal place} \\
\times\ \ 2{\cdot}4 & \text{1 decimal place} \\
\hline
5\,544 & \text{adding gives 2 decimal places}
\end{array}
$$

The answer is 55·44

Dividing decimals

The easiest way is to write each number as a fraction and then use the rules for fractions.

$$23{\cdot}1 \div 2{\cdot}4 = \frac{23{\cdot}1}{2{\cdot}4} \qquad \text{writing as a fraction}$$

$$= \frac{231}{24} \qquad \text{multiplying top and bottom by 10}$$

$$= 9\frac{15}{24} \qquad \text{as a mixed number}$$

$$= 9\frac{5}{8}$$

$$= 9{\cdot}625 \qquad \text{by long division}$$

The whole operation can be done much more easily on a calculator; see p. 225.

Comparing Numbers

To put a list of numbers of different types into increasing or decreasing order, the best way is usually to write them all as decimals first.

Example Write the numbers $2 \cdot 3$, $2\frac{6}{17}$, and $2\frac{13}{40}$ in increasing order.

Answer Writing them all as decimals, using a calculator for example, gives $2 \cdot 3$, $2 \cdot 3529$, $2 \cdot 325$. Ordering these gives $2 \cdot 3$, $2 \cdot 325$, $2 \cdot 3529$. This corresponds to the original numbers in the order $2 \cdot 3$, $2\frac{13}{40}$, $2\frac{6}{17}$.

Powers (also known as Indices)

The numbers 100, 1 000, 10 000 and so on can be written as *powers of* 10. The power counts the number of 0s

$$100 = 10^2 \text{ with power 2}$$

$$1\,000 = 10^3 \text{ with power 3}$$

$$10\,000 = 10^4 \text{ with power 4}$$

10 on its own can be written as 10^1, and 10^0 is taken to be 1. (In fact any number to the power 0 gives 1, see p. 32.)

Powers can be negative as well: $10^{-1} = \frac{1}{10}$, $10^{-2} = \frac{1}{100}$. The minus sign shows that the number is dividing, and so should be written underneath a 1.

Large and small numbers can be written in a more convenient way using powers of ten. For example, writing numbers like 234 000 000 several times during a calculation would be very tedious, and could also cause mistakes through misreading the number. To avoid this the number is written in *standard form*:

$$234\,000\,000 = 2 \cdot 34 \times 10^8$$

The first part is a number between 1 and 10. To get this number the original one had its decimal point moved 8 places. The number of places that it moved is given by the power of 10. If the point moves to the left, then the power is positive. If the point moves to the right, then the power is negative.

Examples *1. 7890 in standard form is $A \times 10^3$. Find A.* (AEB)

Answer $7890 = 7\cdot890 \times 10^3$, writing the first part as a number between 1 and 10. The answer is $A = 7\cdot89$.

  2. 0·0456 in standard form is $4\cdot56 \times 10^n$. Find n. (AEB)

Answer $0\cdot0456 = 4\cdot56 \times 10^{-2}$ (the point moves two places right) so $n = -2$.

As a general rule, if the number is larger than 1 then the power is positive; if the number is less than 1 then the power is negative.

  Numbers in standard form can be multiplied by multiplying the number part and the powers of ten separately. Similarly, when dividing, divide the number parts and powers of 10 separately. Notice that when multiplying powers of ten, the separate powers are *added*. $10^4 \times 10^5 = 10\,000 \times 100\,000 = 1\,000\,000\,000 = 10^9$. When dividing, the powers are *subtracted*. $10^4 \div 10^5 = \frac{10\,000}{100\,000} = \frac{1}{10} = 10^{-1}$.

Example *The distances of the planets Mercury and Neptune from the sun are approximately 6×10^7 km and $4\cdot5 \times 10^9$ km respectively.*

  (a) Find, in standard form, the value of

$$\frac{distance\ of\ Neptune\ from\ the\ sun}{distance\ of\ Mercury\ from\ the\ sun}$$

  (b) Given that the speed of light is 3×10^5 km/s, find, in minutes, the time taken for the light to travel from the sun to Neptune. (LON)

Answer	**Comments**
(a) $\dfrac{4\cdot5 \times 10^9}{6 \times 10^7}$	
$= (4\cdot5 \div 6) \times (10^9 \div 10^7)$	numbers and powers separately
$= 0\cdot75 \times 10^2$	divide numbers, subtract powers
$= 7\cdot5 \times 10^1$	in standard form, moving the decimal place once
(b) Time = Distance ÷ Speed	see p. 100
$= (4\cdot5 \times 10^9) \div (3 \times 10^5)$	
$= (4\cdot5 \div 3) \times (10^9 \div 10^5)$	numbers and powers separately

1

$$= 1.5 \times 10^4$$

divide numbers, subtract
powers

$$= 15\,000 \text{ seconds.}$$

The answer is required in minutes:

$$\text{time} = 15\,000 \div 60 \text{ minutes}$$
$$= 250 \text{ minutes}$$

60 seconds in 1 minute

When adding or subtracting numbers in standard form, you must first convert them back into the ordinary form. You *cannot* just subtract or add the number parts and powers of ten separately.

Example $3.6 \times 10^4 + 6.1 \times 10^5 = 36\,000 + 610\,000$

$$= 646\,000$$

$$= 6.46 \times 10^5 \text{ in standard form}$$

Section 2: Percentages and Ratios

Percentages

A per cent (%) is a fraction where the denominator is 100, so that 20% is the fraction $\frac{20}{100}$, 12·5% is the fraction $\frac{12\cdot5}{100} = \frac{125}{1000}$. To find a percentage of a number, multiply the number by the corresponding fraction of 100.

Example Find 20% of 120.

$$\textbf{Answer} \quad 20\% \text{ of } 120 = \frac{20}{100} \times 120$$

$$= \frac{20 \times 120}{100}$$

$$= \frac{2\,400}{100}$$

$$= 24$$

To express a given fraction as a percentage, multiply the fraction by 100.

Example Express 3 out of 8 as a %.

$$\textbf{Answer} \quad 3 \text{ out of } 8 = \tfrac{3}{8} \text{ which is } \tfrac{3}{8} \times 100\%$$

$$= \frac{300}{8}\%$$

$$= 37\cdot5\%$$

10% is one tenth, 20% is one fifth, 25% is one quarter, 50% is a half and 100% is the whole amount.

Percentages arise in problems dealing with taxes, discounts, profits, stocks and shares and interest rates. Usually they involve finding percentage increases and decreases.

Percentage increase

The total after an increase can be found in two ways. One way is to calculate the increase and then add it on to the original amount. For example, increasing 25 by 20%:

The increase is 20% of $25 = \frac{20}{100} \times 25 = \frac{500}{100} = 5$.

Adding this on to the original 25 gives a total of 30.

The second way is to add on the % increase to 100%, and then find this total % of the original number.

Increasing 25 by 20%, the total % is $100 + 20 = 120\%$. 120% of 25 is $\frac{120}{100} \times 25 = \frac{3000}{100} = 30$ as before. (Notice that this is the same as multiplying by 1·2.)

Percentage decrease

This can be found in the same way, but the % decrease is subtracted from the original amount. For example, decreasing 25 by 10%:

The decrease is 10% of $25 = 2\cdot5$.

Subtracting this from the original 25 gives 22·5 as the answer.

Doing this the second way by subtracting the 10% first from 100%, the remaining % is 90. 90% of $25 = \frac{90}{100} \times 25 = \frac{2250}{100} = 22\cdot5$.

Sometimes the result of a decrease or increase is given, and you have to find out what the original amount was.

Example *The price of an article, after being increased by a tax of 10%, is £3.30. The price before the tax was added was A £0.30 B £0.33 C £2.97 D £3.00 E £3.63* (LON)

Answer After an increase of 10%, the total % is 110%.

So $\qquad\qquad\qquad\qquad 3\cdot30 = 110\%$ of the price

$$3\cdot30 = \frac{110}{100} \text{ of the price}$$

Dividing by 110, $\qquad\qquad \frac{3\cdot30}{110} = \frac{1}{100} \text{ of the price} = 1\%$

$$\frac{3\cdot30}{110} \times 100 = 100\%$$

The original price was $\dfrac{3\cdot30}{110} \times 100 = \dfrac{330}{110} = 3$

so the price was £3.00,   answer = D

Examination questions and examples

In these questions, it is very important to set out the answers neatly and clearly. You are far less likely to make a mistake if you do this, and it is much easier for the examiner to follow your working. Even a correct answer which appears on your paper as though plucked from the air will get no marks for method!

1. A man buys a ticket for a concert for £2.50. He then sells it for £2.35. Calculate the percentage loss that he made on the transaction.

Answer	**Comments**
Loss = £2.50 − £2.35	
= £0.15	loss = original price − final price

The loss is £0.15 out of £2.50

As a fraction this is $\frac{0\cdot15}{2\cdot50}$. As a %

the loss is $\frac{0\cdot15}{2\cdot50} \times 100 = 6\%$.   multiply by 100 for a %
The loss is 6%.   express the answer in words

2. *A café offers lunch at a basic price of £2.50 excluding coffee, which costs 30p. A service charge of 10% is added to the bill. V A T is then charged at 15% of the total. How much, to the nearest penny, would a party of 3 people have to pay if 2 of them had coffee? If the basic cost of the lunch is increased to £3 and the price of coffee remains at 30p, by what percentage, to the nearest whole number, would the bill for the 3 people be increased?* (OXF)

Answer   **Comments**

3 people at £2.50 = £7.50	3 lunches in £s
2 coffees at £0.30 = £0.60	
total = £8.10	
Service at 10% = £0.81	10% = 1 tenth
total = £8.91	add

V A T at 15%   = £1.34   calculator, for example
        total = £10.25
The party would have to pay £10.25 (to nearest penny).

When the charge is increased:
3 people at £3.00 = £9.00
2 coffees at £0.30 = £0.60
        total = £9.60
Service at 10%   = £0.96
        total = £10.56
V A T at 15%   = £1.58
        total = £12.14
The cost at the increased rate would be £12.14.
Increase in cost   = £12.14 − £10.25
             = £1.89
The increase is 1·89 in 10·25
which is a fraction $\frac{1\cdot89}{10\cdot25}$
The percentage increase is $\frac{1\cdot89}{10\cdot25} \times 100$ convert to %
           $= \frac{189}{10\cdot25}$
           $= 18\%$ division done by calculator
The percentage increase is 18%.

Each item is clearly marked, and the calculations are written so that each line follows on from the previous one. Can you see why the service charge and V A T were not added to give a total of 25% increase on the bill?

The next question is about local government rates, which are a form of local tax to raise money for amenities. The rate is given as so many pence in the £, and you interpret it as a %. To find the revenue from the rates, multiply by the rateable value (which is given in the question).

3. *The total sum spent annually on local services by a borough can be called the borough expenses. Such expenses are partly obtained from the rates and partly from the government. In 1980, the total rateable value in a certain borough was £3 600 000 and the rate levied was 90p in the pound.*

In 1980, the government paid 55% of the borough expenses, the rest being obtained from the rates.

Calculate for 1980,
(i) The sum raised by the rates.
(ii) The borough expenses.

In 1981 the total rateable value in this borough remained unchanged but the borough expenses rose by 10%. In 1981, the government paid 60% of the borough expenses. Calculate the rate, in pence per £, levied in 1981. (AEB)

Answer	**Comments**

(i) Rate = 90p in the £ = 90%   rate is a %
     Rates = 90% of £3 600 000

$$= \frac{90}{100} \times 3\,600\,000$$

$$= \frac{90 \times 3\,600\,000}{100} \text{ pounds}$$

$$= £3\,240\,000$$

The sum raised by the rates was £3 240 000 in 1980.

(ii) The government paid 55%, so that 45% was raised from the rates.
£3 240 000 = 45% of total
£3 240 000 ÷ 45 = 1% of total

$$£\frac{3\,240\,000 \times 100}{45} = 100\%$$

The total expenses are

$$£\frac{324\,000\,000}{45} = £7\,200\,000$$

In 1981, the increase in the total
expenditure is 10%
10% of £7 200 000 is £720 000   dividing by 10
The total was 7 200 000

$$\frac{720\,000\,+}{7\,920\,000}$$

So the amount raised by the rates
was
40% of 7 920 000   government paid 60% leaving 40%

$$= £\frac{40}{100} \times 7\,920\,000$$

$$= £3\,168\,000$$

As a fraction of the rateable value
this is $\frac{3168000}{3600000} = 0.88$ by calculator

So the % rate is 0.88×100
The rate levied in 1981 was 88%, or 88p in the £.

Ratios (e.g. 2:3)

Dividing a number up in a given ratio means cutting it into parts. If
the ratio is 2:3, then if two units fit into the smaller one, three units
will fit into the larger one.
Dividing 10 in the ratio 2:3

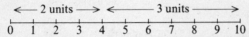

Two units fit on to the smaller piece, three into the larger one. So there
must be five units altogether, each of length 2. The pieces must be 4 (two
units) and 6 (three units).

There is a general method for dividing a number in a given ratio based
on this idea of splitting into units:

  (i) Add the ratios
  (ii) Divide each of the ratio numbers by this total, giving fractions
  (iii) Find these fractions of the number given

Example Divide 200 in the ratio 1:3:6

  (i) $1 + 3 + 6 = 10$
  (ii) dividing the ratios by 10 gives the fractions $\frac{1}{10}, \frac{3}{10}, \frac{6}{10}$
  (iii) The parts are

$$\frac{1}{10} \text{ of } 200 = 20$$

$$\frac{3}{10} \text{ of } 200 = 60$$

$$\frac{6}{10} \text{ of } 200 = 120$$

As a check, notice that the three numbers add up to 200.

Since ratios are very similar to fractions, they have the same property whereby you can multiply or divide all parts by the same amount without changing the value, so $1:2:3$, $3:6:9$, $\frac{1}{3}:\frac{2}{3}:1$ all represent the same ratios.

Example

A jug contains a mixture of water and milk, in the ratio $1:4$ by volume. The density of water is 1 g/cm^3, and the density of the milk is $1\cdot2$ g/cm^3. Calculate the mass of $1\,500$ cm^3 of the liquid.

Answer	Comments
$1\,500$ cm^3 of liquid contains $\frac{1}{5}$ water	divide $1\,500$ in the ratio $1:4$ in fractions $\frac{1}{5}$ and $\frac{4}{5}$
$\frac{1}{5} \times 1\,500 = 300$; there are 300 cm^3 of water. 1 cm^3 has mass 1 g, so 300 cm^3 has mass 300 g.	density 1 g/cm^3
There are $1\,200$ cm^3 of milk, with	$1\,500 - 300 = 1\,200$ density $1\cdot2$ g/cm^3
mass $1\,200 \times 1\cdot2$ g $= 1\,440$ g.	$1440 + 300$
Total mass of liquid $= 1\,740$ g.	

Averages

The average of a set of numbers is their total divided by the number of numbers. The average $1, 4, 3, 6$ and 2 is $\frac{1+4+3+6+2}{5} = \frac{16}{5} = 3\cdot2$.

Example *The average of $\frac{1}{4}$ and $\frac{1}{3}$ is:*
   $A \; \frac{1}{6} \; B \; \frac{2}{7} \; C \; \frac{7}{24} \; D \; \frac{7}{12}$ (AEB)

Answer $\text{Average} = \dfrac{\text{total}}{2}$

$\qquad\qquad \text{total} \;\; = \dfrac{1}{4} + \dfrac{1}{3}$

$\qquad\qquad\qquad\quad = \dfrac{3}{12} + \dfrac{4}{12}$ \qquad make denominators the same

$\qquad\qquad\qquad\quad = \dfrac{7}{12}$

$\qquad\quad \text{Average} = \dfrac{7}{12} \div 2$

$$= \frac{7}{12} \times \frac{1}{2} = \frac{7}{24}$$ remember to $\div$ by 2

The answer is C.

Section 3: Types of Numbers

The natural numbers and integers were introduced in Section 1. A special type of natural number is a *prime number*. A prime number is one that has no factors apart from 1 and itself.

Examples The first few primes are
$$2, 3, 5, 7, 11, 13, 17, 19, 23, 29, 31, 37, 41, 43, 47, \ldots$$

All other numbers can be expressed in terms of their *prime factors*. These are their factors that are also primes. The prime factors of 50, for example, are 2 and 5. 50 can be written as $50 = 2 \times 5 \times 5$, as a product of its prime factors.

Any number that has 2 as a factor is called an *even number*; a number that cannot be divided by 2 is called an *odd number*.

Evens 2, 4, 6, 8, 10, ...
Odds 1, 3, 5, 7, 9, ...

Fractions are sometimes called *rational numbers* (*rational* as in ratio). There are some numbers that cannot be written as fractions, and these are called *irrational numbers*. Some examples of them are given later (p. 32), but first consider:

Squares and Square Roots

Multiplying a number by itself gives its *square*: 4 squared is 4×4, which can be written as 4^2, using the power notation of p. 19. The squares of the first few natural numbers are

Number	0	1	2	3	4	5	6	7	8	9
Square	0	1	4	9	16	25	36	49	64	81

The square of a negative number turns out to be positive:

$$(-2)^2 = (-2) \times (-2)$$
$$= (-)(-)(2 \times 2)$$
$$= +4, \text{ as } -(-) = +$$

Reversing the process gives the *square root*. The square root of a number is the quantity that would have to be squared to give that number. So the square root of 16 is 4, since $4^2 = 16$. Square root is written as $\sqrt{}$.
$\sqrt{49} = 7$, $\sqrt{100} = 10$.

If the square root of a number is an integer, then that number is called a *perfect square* (like 4, 9, 16, ...). It turns out that if the root of a number is not an integer, then it is not even a fraction. This means that $\sqrt{2}$, $\sqrt{3}$, $\sqrt{5}$ and so on are irrational numbers.

Squares and square roots can be found from a calculator or from tables (see p. 222).

When finding a power or root of a fraction, deal with the top and bottom separately. For example:

$$\left(\frac{1}{2}\right)^2 = \frac{1^2}{2^2} = \frac{1}{4}$$

$$\sqrt{\frac{4}{9}} = \frac{\sqrt{4}}{\sqrt{9}} = \frac{2}{3}$$

For decimals, you can first convert them to fractions and then continue as above.

$$(0\cdot002)^2 = \left(\frac{2}{1\,000}\right)^2 = \frac{4}{1\,000\,000}$$

$$= 0\cdot000004$$

$$\sqrt{0\cdot64} = \frac{\sqrt{64}}{\sqrt{100}}$$

$$= \frac{8}{10} = 0\cdot8$$

Square root of 2

It was stated above that 2 is an irrational number, it is not a fraction. However, if you find the root of 2 from a calculator, you may get the answer 1·4142135, which can be written as the fraction $\frac{14142135}{10000000}$. This looks like a contradiction!

The answer is that the value obtained from the calculator is not exactly right. Squaring it out gives the result 1·9999998 which is close to but not equal to 2. The calculator figure is an approximation to $\sqrt{2}$, and is allowed to be a rational number. No calculator could give the exact answer, since an infinite number of decimal places would be needed.

Summary of Types of Numbers

Natural numbers	0, 1, 2, 3, 4, 5, 6, 7, 8, 9, ...
Integers	..., −2, −1, 0, 1, 2, 3, ...
Rationals	$\frac{1}{2}, \frac{3}{4}, \frac{1}{3}, -\frac{1}{2}, \frac{3}{5}, \frac{198}{3}, \frac{2}{1}, \ldots$
Irrationals	$\sqrt{2}, \sqrt{3}, \sqrt{5}, \ldots$
Primes	2, 3, 5, 7, 11, 13, 17, 19, ...
Evens	2, 4, 6, 8, ...
Odds	1, 3, 5, 7, 9, ...
Real numbers	are all the numbers put together

More about Powers

Taking the number 2 as an example, $2^2 = 4$ is 2 squared
$$2^3 = 8 \text{ is 2 cubed}$$
$$2^4 = 16 \text{ is 2 to power 4.}$$
If you multiply any of these powers of two together, you add the powers: $2^3 \times 2^4 = 2 \times 2 \times 2 \times 2 \times 2 \times 2 \times 2 = 2^7$ (see p. 20). Dividing, you subtract the powers: $2^5 \div 2^2 = 2^{5-2} = 2^3 = 2 \times 2 \times 2 = 8$.

It is also possible to have negative powers: $2^{-1} = \frac{1}{2}$, $2^{-2} = \frac{1}{2^2} = \frac{1}{4}$, and so on.

$2^0 = 1$ (as $2^0 \times 2^1 = 2^{0+1} = 2^1 = 2$, so that $2^0 \times 2 = 2$, dividing by 2 gives $2^0 = 1$)

Fraction powers are possible: $2^{\frac{1}{2}}, 2^{\frac{3}{4}}$. What does $2^{\frac{1}{2}}$ mean? Try squaring it.

$$2^{\frac{1}{2}} \times 2^{\frac{1}{2}} = 2^{\frac{1}{2} + \frac{1}{2}} = 2^1 = 2$$

so $2^{\frac{1}{2}}$ must be the square root of 2.

In general, the half power of any number is its square root. Similarly, the power $\frac{1}{3}$ is the cube root, that is the number which when raised to the power 3 gives the original number. $8^{1/3} = 2$ since $2^3 = 8$.

Section 4: Using Letters

Formulae and Expressions

A formula is like a machine. Numbers go in one end, a handle is turned and the result comes out at the other end. The numbers put in are represented by letters and are called *variables*, since their values can be changed. The formula contains instructions for combining the numbers together. The instructions are written in the form of a code called *algebra*.

numbers in

coded instructions

result out

$$\frac{2x + y}{3}$$

handle

This code has its own special rules of grammar:

Terms   Letters (printed in italics) and numbers written next to each other are to be multiplied. They form *terms*. The multiplication sign $\times$ is not normally used in algebra.

             A term can be a single letter or number, or a group of them. The order that the letters are written in does not matter, as numbers can be multiplied in any order.

             Usually the number is written first, followed by the letters in alphabetical order.

        Examples of terms: 2, a, $3xyz$.

Powers   The power notation of the last section (p. 32) is used when a letter is multiplied by itself: $xx = x^2$, $xxx = x^3$ and so on. Also $x^{-1} = \frac{1}{x}$, $x^{\frac{1}{2}} = \sqrt{x}$.

Expressions Terms are added or subtracted to make *expressions*, such as $2x^2y + 3ab$ and $5abc - 6a^2c + 2$. (Notice that the terms can contain powers.)

Expressions can themselves be combined by adding and subtracting, but *should be written inside brackets*.

Expressions can also be combined by multiplying and dividing. The division is always written as a fraction:

$$(2x - 3y)(x + 2y) \text{ and } \frac{(2x - 3y)}{(x + 14y)}.$$

Expressions can also have root signs, such as $\sqrt{x + 2}$ and $x - \sqrt{3b}$.

Working out the value of a formula
When you are given the values of the variables (letters), they can be substituted into the formula. The rules are:

Step 1 Insert the values of the letters, *putting them in brackets*
Step 2 Work out the values of the terms
Step 3 Work out the values of the separate expressions
Step 4 Combine the expression values together

Brackets are used to avoid confusion, for example if the values $a = 1$, $b = 2$, $c = 3$ are to be put into the formula abc, writing (1)(2)(3) reminds you to multiply. If you just write 123, it could be taken for one hundred and twenty-three.

Brackets are particularly useful when the numbers are negative; they remind you to use the rules for combining signs (p. 11).

$(-1)(2)(-3) = (-)(-)(1)(2)(3) = +6.$

Examination questions and examples
Always write each step of the calculation!

1. Given that $p = -3$ and $q = 2$ then $p^2 - pq =$
A −15   B −3   C 0   D 3   E 15   (LON)

Answer   **Comments**

$p^2 - pq = pp - pq$ write powers as multiplication
$\quad = (-3)(-3) - (-3)(2)$ put in the numbers in brackets
$\quad = (-)(-)(3)(3) - (-)(3)(2)$ split off the signs

$$= +9 + 6 \qquad\qquad -(-) = +$$
$$= 15$$

The answer is E.

2. If $a = b + \frac{2}{c}$, calculate a when $b = 2\frac{1}{3}$ and $c = 1\frac{1}{2}$.

Answer	**Comments**
$b = 2\frac{1}{3} = \frac{7}{3}$	change mixed numbers to fractions
$c = 1\frac{1}{2} = \frac{3}{2}$	
So $\dfrac{2}{c} = 2 \div \dfrac{3}{2}$	
$\qquad = 2 \times \dfrac{2}{3}$	see p. 14
$\qquad = \dfrac{4}{3}$	
So $a = \dfrac{7}{3} + \dfrac{4}{3} = \dfrac{11}{3} = 3\dfrac{2}{3}$.	convert to mixed number

3. Given that $p = \frac{1}{3}$ and $q = -2$, calculate the values of (a) $p^2 + q^2$ (b) $(p + q)^2$ (AEB)

Answer	**Comments**
(a) $p^2 + q^2 = pp + qq$	convert powers
$\qquad = \left(\dfrac{1}{3}\right)\left(\dfrac{1}{3}\right)$ $\qquad\quad + (-2)(-2)$	put in numbers
$\qquad = \dfrac{1 \times 1}{3 \times 3}$ $\qquad\quad + (-)(-)(2)(2)$	work out terms
$\qquad = \dfrac{1}{9} + 4$	$-(-) = +$

$$= \frac{1}{9} + \frac{36}{9}$$ write 4 as a fraction

$$= \frac{37}{9}$$ add tops

(b) $(p + q)^2 = (p + q)(p + q)$

$$= \left(\frac{1}{3} + (-2) \right) \left(\frac{1}{3} + (-2) \right)$$

$$= \left(\frac{1}{3} - \frac{6}{3} \right) \left(\frac{1}{3} - \frac{6}{3} \right)$$ write 2 as $\frac{6}{3}$ (see p. 13)

$$= \left(-\frac{5}{3} \right) \left(-\frac{5}{3} \right)$$ work out expressions

$$= \frac{25}{9}$$ as $-(-) = +$

4. *When $x = 10$, the value of $\frac{3}{4}(x - 2) - \frac{1}{2}(2 - x)$*
   is A 2 B 10 C 11 D 12 E 13 (LON)

Answer **Comments**

Put $x = 10$ into expression

$$\frac{3}{4}(10 - 2) - \frac{1}{2}(2 - 10)$$ work out expressions in brackets first

$$= \frac{3}{4}(8) - \frac{1}{2}(-8)$$

$$= \frac{3 \times 8}{4} - (-)\frac{1 \times 8}{2}$$

$$= \frac{24}{4} + \frac{8}{2}$$ $-(-) = +$

$$= 6 + 4$$

$$= 10$$

The answer is B.

Simplifying and Factorizing (Using Brackets)

The expression formed as a combination of other expressions is often quite complicated. Mistakes are easy to make when handling complicated expressions, so it is better to try to simplify them.

The techniques for simplifying are (i) removing brackets; (ii) combining like terms.

How to multiply out brackets

A $+$ sign in front of a pair of brackets has no effect, whereas a $-$ sign changes the signs of all the terms inside the brackets. A letter, number, term or expression written next to a pair of brackets *multiplies* all of the terms inside the brackets.

Examples (a) $2 + (a + b) = 2 + a + b$ brackets can be removed with no effect

      (b) $2 - (x - y) = 2 - x + y$ change signs

      (c) $2a(x - y) = 2ax - 2ay$ multiply the terms by $2a$

      (d) $-x(2x + 1) = -x2x - x$ multiply and change signs

               $= -2xx - x$

               $= -2x^2 - x$ write as power

Expressions can be multiplied out with these methods.

Example $(x + y)(2x - y) = (x + y)2x - (x + y)y$

The first set of brackets is treated as a single term, which then multiplies both of the terms $2x$ and y of the second brackets. The resulting expression still has two sets of brackets, but these can be removed by multiplying by the $2x$ and y which are next to them.

$$(x + y)2x - (x + y)y = x2x + y2x - xy - yy$$

Notice that the $-$ sign in front of the second set of brackets has changed the signs. Simplifying further

$$2xx + 2xy - xy - yy = 2x^2 + xy - y^2$$

The last step involved writing $2xy - xy$ as xy. Both $2xy$ and xy have exactly the same letters, and are called *like terms*. They can be combined by subtracting the number parts. None of the terms are now alike, the expression cannot be simplified further.

Other examples of combining like terms:

$7a^2b + 8a^2b = 15a^2b$ the powers *must* be the same in each term

$-3x^2y^2z + 6x^2y^2z = 3x^2y^2z$

But $7ab - 8ab^2$ *cannot* be simplified further, since the powers differ.

Putting brackets in – factorizing

A factor of an expression is a term that divides the expression exactly. The expression $2a^2b$, for example, has 2, $2a$, a, a^2, b and so on as factors. A quantity that is a factor of more than one expression is said to be a *common factor* of the expressions. An expression can often be written as a product of factors, and is then said to be *factorized*.

Examples (i) $x^2 + 3x$

x^2 can be written as xx, giving $xx + 3x$.

From this you can see that x is a common factor of the two terms. Write this common factor outside a set of brackets $x(\quad)$. Now divide out the factor x from the terms of the original expression $x\!\!\!/x + 3\!\!\!/x$ leaving $x + 3$. Put this into the brackets so that the factorized form of the expression is $x(x + 3)$.

(ii) $2a^2b + 4ab^2$

Writing the powers as repeated multiplication gives $2aab + 4abb$. The common factors are 2, a and b (do not forget the numerical factor). So the first step is to put them outside brackets:

$$2ab(\qquad).$$

Divide these factors out from the expression

$$\overset{2}{\cancel{2}a\cancel{a}b} + \overset{}{\cancel{4}a\cancel{b}b} = a + 2b$$

Put this expression into the brackets

$$2ab(a + 2b)$$

is the required factorization.

(iii) The expression could have more than two terms, for example

$$2p^2q + 4pq^2 + 6pqr$$

which can first be written as

$$2ppq + 4pqq + 6pqr$$

Common factors are 2, p and q so $2pq($ $)$.
Dividing out gives

$$\overset{2}{2\not{p}p\not{q}} + \overset{3}{4\not{p}q\not{q}} + \overset{}{6\not{p}\not{q}r} = p + 2q + 3r$$

Putting this into the brackets gives $2pq(p + 2q + 3r)$ as the factorized form.

If any terms such as bb or xxx are left in the brackets, write them as b^2 and x^3, in power notation.

Sometimes the expression in brackets can be factorized as well. The method used depends on the type of expression.

Type 1 An even number of terms, with pairs of terms having common factors.

Example $ab + 3ac + 2xb + 6xc$
ab and $3ac$ have the factor a in common, so the pair can be factorized as $a(b + 3c)$. $2xb$ and $6xc$ have the factors 2 and x in common, and can be factorized as $2x(b + 3c)$. The whole expression becomes $a(b + 3c) + 2x(b + 3c)$. The term in brackets is a factor common to the two parts of the expression. Take this factor outside a pair of brackets. $(b + 3c)(a + 2x)$ is the factorized form required.

Summary   Pair terms with common factors; the part of each pair left after dividing out is then a factor of the whole expression.

Type 2 The difference of two squares. This has the form

$$(\text{expression})^2 - (\text{expression})^2.$$

Each expression could be a single letter, as in

$a^2 - b^2$. This factorizes as
$$a^2 - b^2 = (a - b)(a + b)$$

To see this, multiply the brackets out:

$$\begin{aligned}(a - b)(a + b) &= (a - b)a + (a - b)b \\ &= aa - ab + ab - bb \\ &= a^2 - b^2 \text{ since the } ab \text{ terms cancel.}\end{aligned}$$

(a and b could be replaced by any expression.)
Note that $x^2 - 4$ is Type 2; $x^2 - 4x$ is Type 1.

Type 3 Quadratic expressions. Quadratic means that there is a power of 2 in the expression. The expression has 3 terms.

Examples $2x^2 - 3x + 1$, $x^2 - 2x + 1$, $5x^2 + 3x - 26$

x is not the only letter than can be used; a quadratic expression can be written in terms of any letter.

Method: taking $2x^2 - 3x + 1$ as an example:

(i)   Write down two pairs of brackets with xs in $(\ \ x\ \ )(\ \ x\ \ )$. Leave spaces for numbers and signs.

(ii)   Write the coefficient of x^2 as a product of two factors. In this case the number is 2 which can only be factored as 2×1. Put these numbers in front of the xs in the brackets: $(2x\ \ )(x\ \ )$.

(iii)   Write the constant term (the one without xs in) as a product of two factors. Here it is 1, which can only be written as 1×1. Put these numbers in the spaces: $(2x\ \ 1)(x\ \ 1)$.

(iv)   Now for the signs. Look at the signs in front of the constant term. A $+$ factorizes as $(+)(+)$ or as $(-)(-)$. A $-$ factorizes as $(+)(-)$ or $(-)(+)$.

If the constant term has a $+$ and the middle term a $+$, then the signs are both $+$. If the middle term is $-$, then the signs are both $-$.

If the constant term is $-$, then the signs are $+$ and $-$. In this example the signs must be both $-$. Putting them in gives $(2x - 1)(x - 1)$.

Always check the answer by multiplying the brackets out to see if you get back to the original expression.

In the case when the two signs have to be a $+$ and a $-$, try them in one order, multiply out and check with the original expression. If it is wrong, swap the signs round and check again.

Sometimes the numbers will have several different ways of factorizing. You will have to try each way until you get the right one. One way of checking the factorizing quickly is with the diagram

$$
\begin{aligned}
2x - 1 &= -x \\
x - 1 &= -2x \\
\hline
&\ -3x
\end{aligned}
$$

The arrows indicate multiplying, and the two products should add up to the middle term of the original expression; the sign should also match.

In the next example there are several ways to arrange the factors.

Example Factorize the quadratic expression $5x^2 + 3x - 26$.

(i) The factors of 5 are 5 and 1.

(ii) The factors of 26 are 1 and 26 *or* 2 and 13. Choose the pair of factors that are closest together, 2 and 13.

(iii) The factors of $-$ and $+$ are $-$. Try the arrangement

$$
\begin{aligned}
5x + 2 &= 2x \\
x - 13 &= \underline{-65x} \\
& -63x
\end{aligned}
$$

This is not the right answer, which should be $+3x$.
Swap the 2 and 13 round:

$$
\begin{aligned}
5x + 13 &= 13x \\
x - 2 &= \underline{-10x} \\
& +3x
\end{aligned}
$$

which is correct. The required factorization is

$$5x^2 + 3x - 26 = (5x + 13)(x - 2)$$

In the example $4x^2 + 8x - 12$, the factor 4 should be divided out first:

$$4(x^2 + 2x - 3)$$

The expression in brackets can then be factorized as above:

$$4(x + 3)(x - 1).$$

The process is quite complicated, but becomes easier with practice. Briefly, the method is:

(i) Remove any numerical common factor
(ii) Factorize the x^2 number
(iii) Factorize the constant number
(iv) Factorize the sign of the constant
(v) Try arrangements until the result checks with the middle term by cross multiplying.

Letters in Fractions

Division of expressions is always written as a fraction, for example $\frac{ax + 3}{x + b}$.
All the rules for fractions introduced for numbers in Section 2 hold for

these fractions with letters. In particular, the top and bottom of the fraction can be multiplied or divided by the same amount without altering its value. This means that the fractions $\frac{a}{b}$, $\frac{2a}{2b}$, $\frac{abc}{b^2c}$ are all the same.

This property is used to put fractions in *lowest terms* (see p. 13).

Example Write the fraction $\dfrac{2a^2bc}{6acd}$ in its lowest terms.

The powers should be written as multiplications first

$$\frac{2aabc}{6acd}$$

Then divide out the common numerical factor 2

$$\frac{aabc}{3acd}$$

Now divide out any letters that appear both top and bottom, they are a and c

$$\frac{\cancel{a}ab\cancel{c}}{3\cancel{a}\cancel{c}d}$$

The result is $\dfrac{ab}{3d}$.

When the powers involved are very high, the rules for powers can be used (see p. 32).

When the fraction involves expressions, *they must be factorized first*. You cannot divide out any terms until this has been done.

Example Write in its lowest terms

$$\frac{2a^2x + 3ax^2}{bx^2 - ax^3}$$

First get rid of the powers

$$\frac{2aax + 3axx}{bxx - axxx}$$

Factorize the top: common factors are a and x. Dividing them leaves $2a\cancel{a}\cancel{x} + 3\cancel{a}\cancel{x}x = 2a + 3x$.

The top factorizes as $ax(2a + 3x)$

Factorize the bottom: common factors are x and x. Dividing them leaves $b\cancel{x}\cancel{x} - ax\cancel{x}\cancel{x} = b - ax$. The bottom factorizes as $xx(b - ax)$.

The fraction can be written as

$$\frac{ax(2a + 3x)}{xx(b - ax)}$$

Now divide out factors common to top and bottom, but do not touch anything inside the brackets

$$\frac{a\cancel{x}(2a + 3x)}{x\cancel{x}(b - ax)}$$

The final result is the fraction

$$\frac{a(2a + 3x)}{x(b - ax)}$$

Fractions can be combined by adding, subtracting, multiplying and dividing, just as can the numerical fractions of Section 1.

$+$ and $-$ When the bottom terms (known as *denominator*) are the same, then the tops (known as *numerator*) are added or subtracted:

$$\frac{a}{x} - \frac{b}{x} = \frac{a-b}{x}$$

When the bottom expressions are different, they can be made the same by multiplying by suitable factors:

$$\frac{a}{x} + \frac{b}{y} = \frac{ay}{xy} + \frac{bx}{xy}$$

$$= \frac{ay + bx}{xy}$$

$\times$ and $\div$ When multiplying, multiply the tops and bottoms separately:

$$\frac{(2x + 1)}{4} \times \frac{3x}{y} = \frac{3x(2x + 1)}{4y}$$

When dividing by a fraction, turn it upside down and multiply:

$$\frac{2x}{z} \div \frac{(x-1)}{3} = \frac{2x}{z} \times \frac{3}{(x - 1)}$$

$$= \frac{6x}{z(x - 1)}$$

Some factorizations to learn and rehearse

$ab + ac = a(b + c)$
$a - b = -(b - a)$
$a^2 - b^2 = (a - b)(a + b)$
$a^2 + 2ab + b^2 = (a + b)^2$
$a^2 - 2ab + b^2 = (a - b)^2$

Examination questions

1. Factorize (a) $2pq^2 - 10pq$
   (b) $2a^2 - 18$
   (c) $4x^2 + 12x + 9$ (AEB)

Answer

(a) $2pq^2 - 10pq = 2pqq - 10pq$
$\quad\quad\quad\quad\quad = 2pq(q - 5)$

(b) $2a^2 - 18 = 2(a^2 - 9)$
$\quad\quad\quad\quad = 2(a^2 - 3^2)$
$\quad\quad\quad\quad = 2(a - 3)(a + 3)$

(c) $\quad 4x^2 + 12x + 9$
$\quad = (2x + 3)(2x + 3)$
$\quad = (2x + 3)^2$

CHECK $(2x + 3)(2x + 3)$
$\quad = (2x + 3)2x + (2x + 3)3$
$\quad = 2x2x + 3(2x) + 2x3 + 3(3)$
$\quad = 4x^2 + 6x + 6x + 9$
$\quad = 4x^2 + 12x + 9 \quad correct$

Comments

first take out common factors
$2p\cancel{q}q - 1\cancel{0}p\cancel{q}$
2 is a common factor
$9 = 3^2$, difference of square
using the general formula
(*see p.* 40)
quadratic!
$4 = 2 \times 2 \quad 9 = 3 \times 3$
$+ = +(+)$

2. $ap + by - pb - ay$ can be expressed as
   $A\ (a + b)(p - y) \quad B\ (a - b)(p - y) \quad C\ (a - b)(y - p) \quad D\ (a + b)(y - p)$
   $E\ (b - a)(p - y)$ (LON)

Answer

$\quad ap + by - pb - ay$
$= ap - pb + by - ay$
$= p(a - b) + y(b - a)$
$= p(a - b) - y(a - b)$
$= (p - y)(a - b)$
$= (a - b)(p - y)$ answer **B**

Comments

four terms, factorize in pairs

$(b - a) = -(a - b)$
$(a - b)$ is common factor

3. (a) Simplify (i) $(x + y)^2 - (x + y)(x - y) + (x - y)^2$

  (ii) $\dfrac{x + 2y}{x^2 - 4y^2}$

  (b) *Factorize* $x^2 + 2x - 24$ (OXF)

Answer **Comments**

(a, i) $(x + y)(x + y) - (x + y)(x - y)$ get rid of powers
  $+ (x - y)(x - y)$
  $= x(x + y) + y(x + y) - (x^2 - y^2)$
  $+ x(x - y) - y(x - y)$ multiply out brackets.
  $= xx + xy + yx + yy - x^2 + y^2$ Middle term is difference
  $+ xx - xy - yx + yy$ of squares
  $= x^2 + xy + xy + y^2 - x^2 + y^2$ be careful with minuses
  $+ x^2 - xy - xy + y^2$
  $= x^2 + 3y^2$ adding like terms

(ii) $\dfrac{x + 2y}{x^2 - 4y^2} = \dfrac{x + 2y}{(x - 2y)(x + 2y)}$ denominator is difference
  of squares, $x^2 - 4y^2 =$
  $x^2 - (2y)^2$
  dividing the common

  $= \dfrac{1}{x - 2y}$ factor $(x + 2y)$
  $24 = 4 \times 6, - = (-)(+)$

(b) $x^2 + 2x - 24 = (x - 4)(x + 6)$

4. *Simplify as far as possible* $\dfrac{6a^2}{5c^3} \div \dfrac{3a}{20c^2}$ (AEB)

Answer **Comments**

$= \dfrac{6a^2}{5c^3} \times \dfrac{20c^2}{3a}$ turn and multiply

$= \dfrac{120aacc}{15ccca}$ multiply tops and
  bottoms

$= \dfrac{8a}{c}$ divide out by 15*cca*

Rearranging Formulae and Solving Equations

The value of a formula changes with different numbers being put in. It is itself a variable, and can be denoted by a letter. For example $y = \frac{2x+1}{3}$. The instructions can be written out as a *flow diagram*:

$$x \longrightarrow \boxed{\times 2} \longrightarrow \boxed{+1} \longrightarrow \boxed{\div 3} \longrightarrow y$$

means	$\times$ by 2	add 1	divide by 3
effect	$2x \longrightarrow$	$2x + 1 \longrightarrow$	$\dfrac{2x+1}{3}$

Each box acts on the result of all the preceding ones.

Sometimes the value of y is known, and the problem is to find what value of x was put in. This would involve reversing the flow of the diagram. To do this, the opposite of each step must be used. The opposite of $\times 2$ is $\div 2$, the opposite of $+1$ is -1, and the opposite of $\div 3$ is $\times 3$.

$$y \longrightarrow \boxed{\times 3} \longrightarrow \boxed{-1} \longrightarrow \boxed{\div 2} \longrightarrow x$$

$$\longrightarrow 3y \qquad \longrightarrow 3y - 1 \longrightarrow \frac{3y-1}{2}$$

So x can be worked out from the formula $x = \frac{3y-1}{2}$. The original formula has been rearranged, to give x in terms of y.

Example   *Make x the subject of the formula $y = \sqrt{\frac{(x^2-7)f}{p}}$* (LON)

Answer
Flow diagram

$$x \longrightarrow \boxed{\text{square}} \longrightarrow \boxed{-7} \longrightarrow \boxed{\times f} \longrightarrow \boxed{\div p} \longrightarrow \boxed{\text{root}} \longrightarrow y$$

Reversing

$$x \longleftarrow \boxed{\text{root}} \longleftarrow \boxed{+7} \longleftarrow \boxed{\div f} \longleftarrow \boxed{\times p} \longleftarrow \boxed{\text{square}} \longleftarrow y$$

$$\sqrt{\frac{py^2}{f} + 7} \qquad \frac{py^2}{f} + 7 \qquad \frac{py^2}{f} \qquad py^2 \qquad y^2 \qquad y$$

$$x = \sqrt{\frac{py^2}{f} + 7}$$

Comment Opposite of $\sqrt{}$ is square. Opposite of $\times p$ is $\div p$

Some formulae have more than one variable, and the flow diagram method *cannot be used*. When this is the case, the formula has to be manipulated until x is isolated on one side. The idea is to get all the xs on one side of the formula, and on the same level.

Example Rearrange $\dfrac{yx - 3}{2y - 3x} = 2$, to give x in terms of y.

Answer
Multiply both sides by $(2y - 3x)$

$$\frac{(2y - 3x)(yx - 3)}{(2y - 3x)} = 2(2y - 3x)$$

Cancel out the common factor $(2y - 3x)$ from the fraction

$$(yx - 3) = 2(2y - 3x)$$

Remove the brackets

$$yx - 3 = 4y - 6x$$

Add 3 to both sides and also add $6x$ to both sides

$$yx - 3 + 3 + 6x = 4y - 6x + 3 + 6x$$

Add like terms

$$yx + 6x = 4y + 3$$

Factorize

$$x(y + 6) = 4y + 3$$

Divide both sides by $(y + 6)$

$$\frac{x(y + 6)}{(y + 6)} = \frac{(4y + 3)}{(y + 6)}$$

Divide out the common factor on the left

$$x = \frac{(4y + 3)}{(y + 6)}$$

Which is the required formula.

All the steps were moving expressions to the left and right of the $=$ sign, and up and down in the fractions, by doing the *same* arithmetic operation to both sides of the $=$ sign.

Examination question

It is given that $p = 2nx - y$.

   (i) *Calculate p when $n = 3$, $x = 4$ and $y = -5$.*

  (ii) *Express y in terms of n, x and p.*

 (iii) *Express n in terms of p, x and y.*

 (iv) *If p, x and y are all doubled, state the effect on n.* (A E B)

Answer	Comments

(i) $p = 2nx - y = 2(3)(4) - (-5)$

$\qquad\qquad = 24 + 5 \qquad\qquad -(-) = +$

$\qquad\qquad = 29$

(ii) $p = 2nx - y$

$\quad p + y = 2nx \qquad\qquad$ move the y by adding y to each side of the equation

$\quad y = 2nx - p \qquad\qquad$ move the p by subtracting p from each side of the equation

(iii) $p = 2nx - y$

$\quad p + y = 2nx$

$\quad 2nx = p + y$

$\quad n = \dfrac{(p + y)}{2x} \qquad\qquad$ divide both sides by $2x$

(iv) First put $p = 1$, $y = 1$, $x = 1$
in the above

$$n = \frac{1 + 1}{2} = 1$$

Now double, so that

$p = 2$, $y = 2$ and $x = 2$

$$n = \frac{2 + 2}{4} = \frac{4}{4} = 1$$

There is no effect on n.

Section 5: Variation and Proportionality ($y \propto x$)

A formula is a very precise way of giving the relationship between variables. It is not always necessary or possible to be so exact. If you measure the length of a metal rod at different temperatures you would find that the rod increases in length by the same amount for each $1°$ temperature increase. The length increase is *proportional* to the temperature increase. If the length increase is represented by the letter L, and the temperature increase by the letter T, then the relation can be written as $L \propto T$, where the $\propto$ sign means 'is proportional to'.

Another way of saying this is that the length increase *varies directly* with temperature increase.

If x and y are general variables, then they can have different kinds of proportionality relations.

$y \propto x$ y is proportional to x (y varies directly as x)

$y \propto x^2$ y is proportional to the square of x

$y \propto x^3$ y is proportional to the cube of x

$y \propto \dfrac{1}{x}$ y is *inversely proportional* to x

$y \propto \dfrac{1}{x^2}$ y is inversely proportional to the square of x

The word 'inversely' tells you that the power of x appears as the denominator.

The proportionality relation can be turned into a formula by using a *constant of proportionality*, usually written as the letter k.

$$y \propto x \quad \text{is written as} \quad y = kx$$

The value of k is found by putting in a pair of values for x and y.

Joint proportionality (also known as *joint variation*) occurs when several variables are involved, for example $V \propto \frac{t^2 L}{m}$ which can also be written as a formula $V = k\frac{t^2 L}{m}$. The constant k can be found by putting in known values of t, L and m.

Examination questions

1. Given that y is inversely proportional to x, and x = 2 when y = 3, then, when y = 1, x =
A 6   B 3   C 2   D 1½   E ⅔(LON)

Answer	**Comments**
$y \propto \dfrac{1}{x}$	*inversely* proportional
So $y = \dfrac{k}{x}$	constant of proportionality
$x = 2 \; y = 3$	
$3 = \dfrac{k}{2}$	
$k = 6$	multiply by 2
So $y = \dfrac{6}{x}$	
When $y = 1$ $1 = \dfrac{6}{x}$	
$1 = \dfrac{x}{6}$	take reciprocal (see p. 15)
$x = 6$	multiply by 6 (see equations p. 53)

The answer is A.

2. Water flows from a pipe into a container at a rate such that the volume of water in the container is proportional to the square of the time. If the volume is V cm^3 at t seconds, and given that $V = 9$ when $t = 2$, calculate the volume of water after 12 seconds.

Answer	**Comments**
$V \propto t^2$	V is proportional to the square of t
$V = kt^2$, and $V = 9$ when $t = 2$	k = constant of proportionality
So $9 = 4k$	

$$k = \frac{9}{4}$$

$$V = \frac{9}{4}t^2$$

Put $t = 12$

$$V = \frac{9}{4} \times 12^2$$

$$= \frac{9 \times 144}{4}$$

$$= 324$$

The volume of water is 324 cm^3 after 12 seconds.

Equations

An *equa*tion involves an *equa*ls sign. On either side of the = are expressions or numbers. The equation represents a condition that the variable must satisfy, and in this respect it is quite different from a formula. A formula gives different numbers out for different numbers put in, while an equation is only satisfied for certain values of the variable. These values are called the *solutions* of the equation, and are usually few in number.

The methods for finding the solutions of equations are very similar to those for rearranging formulae (see pp. 47–50). Take the example $y = \frac{2x-3}{5}$, which has to be rearranged to give an expression for x:

multiply the 5 over	$5y = 2x - 3$
add the 3 across	$5y + 3 = 2x$
divide by 2	$\frac{5y + 3}{2} = x$

which is the required formula.

Now consider the problem of solving the equation $\frac{2x-3}{5} = 7$. This is equivalent to rearranging the formula for the case when y is 7. The steps are exactly the same:

multiply the 5 over	$2x - 3 = 35$
add the 3 across	$2x = 38$
divide by 2	$x = 19$

The solution is $x = 19$. (The *solution set* is $\{19\}$. See p. 177 for an explanation of set notation.)

This is the only value of x that satisfies the condition expressed by the equation. Try putting in any other value of x and you will find that the expression does not have the value of 7.

This example is a case of a *linear equation*, which means that powers of x are not involved (that is, no x^2, x^3 or $\sqrt{}$ terms).

Linear equations can always be solved by this technique of rearranging. Notice also that since x appeared only once in the equation, the flow diagram method (see p. 47) could have been used. When the variable appears several times, the expressions may have to be simplified first:

Example *Solve the equation*

$$\frac{x+2}{3} - \frac{2x-1}{4} = \frac{1}{2} \text{(LON)}$$

The left-hand side should first be written as a single fraction, so multiply top and bottom of the first fraction by 4 and those of the second by 3

$$\frac{4(x+2)}{12} - \frac{3(2x-1)}{12} = \frac{1}{2}$$

Note the brackets, and that the right-hand side has not been changed. Now combine the two fractions by subtracting the tops only:

$$\frac{4(x+2) - 3(2x-1)}{12} = \frac{1}{2}$$

Simplify the top expression by removing the brackets

$$\frac{4x + 8 - 6x + 3}{12} = \frac{1}{2}$$

$$\frac{-2x + 11}{12} = \frac{1}{2}$$

Multiply the 12 *and* the 2 over, called *cross multiplying* (or multiply both sides by 24 and cancel out common factors)

$$2(-2x + 11) = 12$$

Multiply out the brackets $-4x + 22 = 12$

Take the 22 over $-4x = 12 - 22$

$$-4x = -10$$

Divide by -4

$$x = \frac{-10}{-4}$$

$$x = 2\cdot5 \; (-(-) = +)$$

The whole equation must be written down at each step, so that the expressions on either side of the $=$ are always actually equal.

Cross multiplying is a useful technique whenever both sides are *single* fractions. $\frac{a}{b} = \frac{c}{d}$ cross multiplies to give $ad = bc$.

Each step of the solution must correspond to multiplying, dividing, adding or subtracting the same quantity on both sides, or to simplifying one of the sides.

Quadratic Equations

These are equations that involve a squared term, like x^2. The simplest type is an equation that has only an x^2 and a number: for example $x^2 = 4$. The solution is found simply by taking the square root of each side of the equation, because the square root of any squared number will be that number itself.

$$x^2 = 4$$

take roots $\qquad x = 2$

However, this is not the only solution, since $(-2)^2 = (-2)(-2)$

$$= (-)(-)(2)(2)$$

$$= 4.$$

$x = -2$ is also a solution. In general, quadratic equations should have two solutions, arising from the fact that numbers have both positive and negative square roots.

Factor method

This depends on the fact that if two numbers multiply to give zero, then at least one of the two numbers must itself be zero (since two non-zero numbers multiply to give a non-zero answer). Applying this to the equation

$$(2x - 6)(x + 1) = 0$$

and noticing that the left-hand side is a product of two expressions and *the right-hand side is zero*, then at least one of the two expressions must be zero:

so $\qquad\qquad 2x - 6 = 0 \quad$ or $\quad x + 1 = 0$

$\qquad\qquad\qquad 2x = 6 \quad$ or $\qquad x = -1$

$\qquad\qquad\qquad x = 3 \quad$ or $\qquad x = -1$

which are the two solutions.

The left-hand side could in fact be a product of any number of expressions. As long as the right-hand side is zero, then a solution is found by putting each of the factors equal to zero:

$$(x + 1)(x - 3)(x - 4) = 0$$

has solutions $x = -1$, $x = 3$ and $x = 4$. This is no longer a quadratic equation, since by multiplying out the brackets you will see that there is an x^3 term as well.

On p. 41 you found out how to factorize quadratic expressions. So you can factorize the left-hand side of a quadratic equation and then use the above method to find the solutions:

Example *Solve the equation $2x^2 - 9x - 5 = 0$* (LON part)

The expression must first be factorized $(2x \qquad)(x \qquad)$
$\qquad\qquad\qquad\qquad\qquad\qquad\qquad (2x \quad 1)(x \quad 5)$
$\qquad\qquad\qquad\qquad\qquad\qquad\qquad (2x + 1)(x - 5)$

(You should work through this factorizing, filling in the steps.)

The equation can then be written as

$$(2x + 1)(x - 5) = 0$$

So, putting each factor $= 0$ in turn

$\qquad\quad 2x + 1 = 0 \quad$ or $\quad x - 5 = 0$

$\qquad\qquad 2x = -1 \qquad\qquad x = 5$

$\qquad\qquad x = -\dfrac{1}{2} \quad$ or $x = 5$ (The solution set is $\{-\frac{1}{2}, 5\}$.)

One word of warning: if the right-hand side is *not* 0, then there is no point in factorizing the left-hand side. The equation $(x + 1)(x - 2) = 3$

cannot be solved by putting one factor $= 1$ and the other $= 3$, for example. You have to multiply out the brackets, put everything on the left, and when there is a 0 on the right you can factorize again.

Example Solve the equation $x(x - 1) = 5$.
Avoiding the trap:
Multiply out the brackets $xx - 1x = 5$
$$x^2 - x = 5$$
subtract the 5 over $x^2 - x - 5 = 0.$

Unfortunately, by no amount of fiddling with factors and signs can the left be easily factorized! If the expression cannot be factorized then you cannot use the factor method. Another way is necessary.

The formula method
The most general quadratic equation can be written in the form $ax^2 + bx + c = 0$, where the *coefficients a, b* and *c* are constant numbers. Any quadratic can be written like this after simplifying and rearranging. The formula giving the solutions is

$$x = \frac{-b \pm \sqrt{(b^2 - 4ac)}}{2a}$$

where the $\pm$ indicates that you should first work through with the $+$ sign, and then with the $-$. In this way two solutions are found.

Example In the example above we ended up with the equation

$$x^2 - x - 5 = 0$$

Read off the values of *a, b* and *c*: $a =$ coefficient of $x^2 = 1$
$$b = \text{coefficient of } x = -1$$
$$c = \text{constant term} = -5$$

Notice that they include the signs as well, *and no xs*. It is a common mistake to put xs into the formula as well!
    Put these numbers into the formula (carefully!)

$$x = \frac{-(-1) \pm \sqrt{(-1)^2 - 4(1)(-5)}}{2(1)}$$

Multiply, using $-(-) = +$

$$x = \frac{1 \pm \sqrt{1 + 20}}{2}$$

$$x = \frac{1 \pm \sqrt{21}}{2}$$

Now you have to look up the square root in tables or use a calculator. Writing in this value $x = \frac{1 \pm 4 \cdot 583}{2}$ taking the answer to 3 decimal places. Splitting the two cases,

$$x = \frac{1 + 4 \cdot 583}{2} \quad \text{or} \quad x = \frac{1 - 4 \cdot 583}{2}$$

So

$$x = \frac{5 \cdot 583}{2} \quad \text{or} \quad x = \frac{-3 \cdot 583}{2}$$

$$x = 2 \cdot 791 \quad \text{or} \quad x = -1 \cdot 791$$

Express the answer to two decimal-place accuracy:

$$x = 2 \cdot 79 \quad \text{or} \quad x = -1 \cdot 79.$$

When you solve an equation, always write down all the details; it is not only expected by the examiner, but also helps you to avoid arithmetical errors. When the formula is used, it will usually be necessary to give the answer to some specified accuracy. Make sure that you do this correctly! Note that in the above example the working used 3 decimal-place accuracy, but the answer was rounded up to two.

Simultaneous Equations

When an equation has two variables in it, then it does not have a single solution: for example, the equation $2x + y = 1$ expresses a condition that can be satisfied by many pairs of values of x and y. In fact, choosing any value for y gives an equation to find the value of x. However, if another similar equation is to be satisfied at the same time (or *simultaneously*) then it turns out that only one pair of values for x and y will do. Suppose the two equations are

$$2x + y = 1 \text{ (i)}$$

and

$$x - y = 5 \text{ (ii)}$$

where the equations are labelled with (i) and (ii) for later reference.

These two equations can be added or subtracted by adding or subtracting the two sides separately. Adding them:

$$2x + y = 1$$
$$+$$
$$\underline{x - y = 5}$$
$$3x \quad\;\; = 6$$

The two y terms have cancelled out, leaving an equation in x only which is easily solved to give the answer $x = 2$. Now, putting this value of x back into either of the original equations will give an equation in y. Putting it into equation (i) for example:

$$4 + y = 1$$
$$y = 1 - 4$$
$$y = -3$$

So the pair of solutions is $x = 2$ and $y = -3$.

The trick was to combine the two equations in some way so that the terms in y cancelled. This can always be done, but the equations sometimes have to be multiplied by suitable factors first.

Example Solve the simultaneous equations $\quad 4x - 3y = 5$ (i)
$$2x + y = 8 \text{ (ii)}$$
Multiplying equation (ii) by 3 gives the result $6x + 3y = 24$ (iii)
The y term is now the same (apart from the $-$) as that in (i), so, adding equations (i) and (iii):

$$4x - 3y = 5$$
$$+$$
$$\underline{6x + 3y = 24}$$
$$10x \quad\;\; = 29$$

Dividing by 10 gives the solution $x = 2 \cdot 9$.
Putting this into equation (ii) gives

$$5 \cdot 8 + y = 8$$
$$y = 8 - 5 \cdot 8$$
$$y = 2 \cdot 2.$$

The solutions are $x = 2 \cdot 9$ and $y = 2 \cdot 2$.
Put these values into equation (i) as a check.

Examination questions and examples

1. Solve the equations (a) $7 - 3p = 2$

$$(b)\ 4q = q^2 \text{(AEB part)}$$

Answer	**Comments**
(a) $7 - 3p = 2$	
$-3p = 2 - 7$	subtract 7 to the right
$-3p = -5$	
$p = \dfrac{-5}{-3}$	divide by -3
$p = \dfrac{5}{3}$	cancel minuses
(b) $\qquad 4q = q^2$	
$q^2 - 4q = 0$	subtract $4q$ over and flip equation to put 0 on the right
$q(q - 4) = 0$	factorize
$q = 0 \quad \text{or} \quad q - 4 = 0$	
$q = 0 \quad \text{or} \quad q = 4$	

2. $3(a + 2) - 4(1 + 2a) = 5(a - 5) + 7(1 - a)$. Find the value of *a*.

Answer	**Comments**
$3a + 6 - 4 - 8a = 5a - 25 + 7 - 7a$	remove the brackets
$-5a + 2 = -2a - 18$	add like terms
$-3a = -20$	add $2a$ to left, and 2 to right
$a = \dfrac{20}{3}$	divide by -3

3. Solve the equation

$$1 + \frac{2}{x - 3} = \frac{5}{9}$$

Answer	Comments
$\dfrac{2}{x-3} = \dfrac{5}{9} - 1$	take 1 to the right
$\dfrac{2}{x-3} = -\dfrac{4}{9}$	make right-hand side a single fraction
$\dfrac{x-3}{2} = -\dfrac{9}{4}$	take reciprocals
$4x - 12 = -18$	cross multiply
$4x = -6$	add 12 over
$x = -1{\cdot}5$	divide by 4

4. $\sqrt{\dfrac{8x}{x-1}} = 4. \ x =$

$A\ 3 \quad B\ 2 \quad C\ \tfrac{1}{2} \quad D\ -\tfrac{1}{3} \quad E\ -1$ (LON)

Answer	Comments
$\dfrac{8x}{x-1} = 16$	square to remove root sign
$8x = 16(x-1)$	cross multiply
$8x = 16x - 16$	Remove brackets
$16 = 16x - 8x$	Put xs on right
$16 = 8x$	
$x = 2$ answer B	

5. Two variables X and Y are such that $pX + qY = 7$ where p and q are constants. When $X = 4$, $Y = 3$ and when $X = 6$, $Y = 15$. Calculate:
   (i) The values of the constants p and q.
   (ii) The value of Y when $X = 2$.
   (iii) The value of X when $X = Y$. (AEB)

Answer	**Comments**

(i) $X = 4$ and $Y = 3$

$$4p + 3q = 7 \text{ (i)}$$

$X = 6$ and $Y = 15$

$6p + 15q = 7 \text{ (ii)}$	
$20p + 15q = 35 \text{ (iii)}$	multiply (i) by 5
$14p = 28$	subtract (ii) from (iii)
$p = 2$	
$8 + 3q = 7$	Substitute into (i)
$3q = -1$	
$q = -\dfrac{1}{3}$	

(ii) Put in these values of p and q

$2X - \dfrac{1}{3}Y = 7$	
$4 - \dfrac{Y}{3} = 7$	$X = 2$
$-\dfrac{Y}{3} = 3$	subtract 4 from both sides
$Y = -9$	multiply by -3

(iii) Put $X = Y$

$2X - \dfrac{X}{3} = 7$	
$\dfrac{6X}{3} - \dfrac{X}{3} = 7$	denominators the same
$\dfrac{6X - X}{3} = 7$	

$$\frac{5X}{3} = 7$$

$$5X = 21 \qquad \text{multiply by 3}$$

$$X = \frac{21}{5} = 4 \cdot 2$$

6. *A car travels x km for every litre of petrol used. Write down an expression for the number of litres used to travel 175 km.*

A second car travels (x + 4) km for every litre of petrol used. Write down an expression for the number of litres this car used to travel 175 km.

Given that the first car used 5 litres of petrol more than the second car for the 175 km journey, write down an equation which x must satisfy. Simplify this equation and show that it reduces to

$$x^2 + 4x - 140 = 0$$

Solve this equation, and hence find the number of litres of petrol used by the second car for the journey. (AEB)

Answer   **Comments**

The number of litres used by the first car was $\frac{175}{x}$.

The number of litres used by the second car was $\frac{175}{x+4}$.

The first car uses 5 litres more

$$\frac{175}{x} = \frac{175}{x+4} + 5$$

So $\dfrac{175}{x} - \dfrac{175}{x+4} = 5$

$$\frac{175(x+4) - 175x}{x(x+4)} = 5 \qquad \text{put over a common denominator}$$

$$175(x+4) - 175x = x(x+4)5 \qquad \text{multiply across}$$

$$175x + 700 - 175x = 5x^2 + 20x \qquad \text{remove brackets}$$

$$700 = 5x^2 + 20x$$
$$5x^2 + 20x - 700 = 0 \qquad \text{make the right-hand side 0}$$
$$x^2 + 4x - 140 = 0 \qquad \text{divide by 5}$$

The left side factorizes,

$$(x + 14)(x - 10) = 0$$

$$x = -14 \text{ or } x = 10$$

Only a positive value is possible, so the answer is $x = 10$.

The number of litres of petrol used by the second car was

$$\frac{175}{x+4} = \frac{175}{10+4} = \frac{175}{14} = 12 \cdot 5 \text{ litres.}$$

Inequalities

An inequality looks like an equation, but instead of an $=$ sign there is a $<$ or a $>$. These signs mean 'is less than' and 'is greater than' respectively.

Example $x < 2$, $y + 2 > 6$, $1 < x < 5$.

Related signs are $\leqslant$ (less than or equal to) and $\geqslant$ (greater than or equal to).

Example $x \leqslant 2$ would include $x = 2$ as a possibility.

To *solve* an inequality is to simplify it so that it is of the form $x < a$ or $x > a$ where a is some number.

Example $2x + 1 < 5$

Subtracting 1 from both sides $2x < 4$
Dividing by 2 $\qquad\qquad\qquad x < 2$

The procedure is very similar to that for simplifying equations. The only important difference is that *when multiplying or dividing by a negative number, the inequality sign is reversed.*

Examples $x \leqslant 1$, $-x \geqslant -1$; $1 < 2$ while $-1 > -2$, multiplying by -1 in both cases.

The solution of an inequality can be shown on a number line, $x < 1$ or $x > 4$ can be shown as

x can be sandwiched between two $<$s, as in $3 < x < 7$, which means that x is between 3 and 7. BUT you cannot write $3 > x > 7$. This says x is greater than 7 and less than 3, both of which cannot be true, so you write it as $x < 7$ or $x > 3$. When joining two inequalities together, the result of covering up the middle term must also be true. $3 < 7$ is true but $3 > 7$ is not.

You show whether the end values of the thickened part of the number line are included in the following way: a ring is put on the end. If the number is included, the ring is filled in, if the number is not included then the ring is left open.

When two inequalities are to be satisfied at the same time, draw two number lines and take the overlapping parts of the two solutions.

Example *Make two copies of the number line*

and indicate, by thickening a part of the line, the solution sets of the inequalities (i) $2x + 1 \leqslant -3$
(ii) $-14 \leqslant 3x - 2$.

Hence find the values of x in the set of integers which satisfy both these inequalities simultaneously. (LON)

Answer	**Comments**
(i) $2x + 1 \leqslant -3$	
$2x \leqslant -4$	subtract 1 over
$x \leqslant -2$	divide by 2
(ii) $-14 \leqslant 3x - 2$	
$-12 \leqslant 3x$	add the 2 over
$-4 \leqslant x$	divide by 3

On the number line

(i)

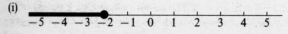

(ii)

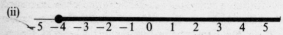

The integers in the overlap region are -4, -3 and -2.

Section 6: Functions and Graphs ($f : x \to \ldots$)

Functions

A formula gives a way of pairing numbers. For example, the formula $y = \frac{2x+1}{3}$ gives $y = 3$ when $x = 4$. The numbers 4 and 3 are paired off.

A procedure for pairing things together is called a *function* or *mapping*. The possible values of x that can be put into the formula may be restricted. If x represents a length, then it must be positive, if it represents the number of items sold in a shop, then it must be a whole number. The set of allowed values of x is called the *domain* of the function. The set of possible values that the formula produces is called the *range* of the function.

A function consists of three parts: *domain*, *range* and a *formula* or rule for pairing numbers.

The f notation is used to give the formula of the function. A function can be written as, for example, $f : x \to x^2 + 1$ (said as 'x goes to $x^2 + 1$') and also in the form $f(x) = x^2 + 1$ (said as 'f of x is $x^2 + 1$').

The variable x can be replaced by a number, for example $f(2) = 2^2 + 1 = 5$, substituting $x = 2$ into the formula. Other letters and also expressions can be used as well. $f(a) = a^2 + 1$, $f(-b) = (-b)^2 + 1 = b^2 + 1$, $f(2x + 1) = (2x + 1)^2 + 1 = 4x^2 + 4x + 1 + 1 = 4x^2 + 4x + 2$. Other letters can be used in place of f, for example g and h.

Examination questions and examples

1. The function f is defined by $f : x \to x^2 - 3$, on the domain of real numbers.

(a) Calculate $f(1 \cdot 2)$ correct to two decimal places.

(b) Find the values of x, correct to two decimal places, for which $f(x) = 0 \cdot 5$.

Answer

(a) $f(1 \cdot 2) = (1 \cdot 2)^2 - 3$

Comments

put $1 \cdot 2$ into the formula

$$= 1 \cdot 44 - 3 \qquad\qquad 1 \cdot 2^2 = 1 \cdot 44$$
$$= -1 \cdot 56$$

(b) $x^2 - 3 = 0 \cdot 5$
$$x^2 = 3 \cdot 5$$
$$x = \pm \sqrt{3 \cdot 5} = \pm 1 \cdot 87 \qquad \text{(calculator)}$$

2. *Given that* $f(x) = \dfrac{2x + 5}{x^2 - 2}$*, the value of* $f(-2)$ *is*

$A \ -\frac{1}{2} \quad B \ -\frac{1}{6} \quad C \ \frac{1}{6} \quad D \ \frac{1}{2} \quad E \ \frac{3}{2}$ (LON)

Answer **Comments**

$$f(-2) = \frac{2(-2) + 5}{(-2)^2 - 2} \qquad\qquad \text{put } x = -2$$

$$= \frac{1}{2} \qquad\qquad\qquad (-2)^2 = 4$$

The answer is D.

3. *Under the mapping* $f: x \to x^2$ *the domain is* $0 \leqslant x \leqslant 9$*, the range is the set of values of* y *given by*

$A \ -3 \leqslant y \leqslant 3 \quad B \ 0 \leqslant y \leqslant 3 \quad C \ -9 \leqslant y \leqslant 9 \quad D \ 0 \leqslant y \leqslant 81 \quad E \ -81 \leqslant y \leqslant 81$ (LON)

Answer **Comments**
$0 \leqslant x \leqslant 9$ see p. 64 about inequalities

$0 \leqslant x^2 \leqslant 81$

$y = x^2$, so the range is

$0 \leqslant y \leqslant 81$, answer D

A function or mapping can be given in other ways besides specifying a formula. A diagram can be used which connects members of the domain with the corresponding members of the range.

Example

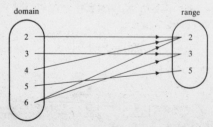

This maps a positive integer to its prime factors (see p. 30).

Examination question

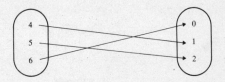

The diagram illustrates a mapping of the domain set {4, 5, 6} onto the range set {0, 1, 2}. What is a possible rule for this mapping?
A $x \rightarrow x - 3$ B $x \rightarrow \frac{x^2 - 7}{9}$ C $x \rightarrow$ remainder when x is divided by 3
D $x \rightarrow$ difference between x and the smallest odd number which is larger than x E No rule could map the given domain onto the given range.
(LON)

Answer

$x \rightarrow x - 3$ would send $6 \rightarrow 3$. But $6 \rightarrow 0$, so A is wrong.

$x \rightarrow \frac{x^2 - 7}{9}$ would send $6 \rightarrow \frac{29}{9}$, but $6 \rightarrow 0$, so B is wrong.

$x \rightarrow$ remainder when x is divided by 3 sends $4 \rightarrow 1$, $5 \rightarrow 2$ and $6 \rightarrow 0$.

This is the correct answer. The answer is C.

Combining functions

Two functions can be combined together to form a new function. If $f(x) = x^2 - 4x$ and $g(x) = x + 2$ (with some suitable domains) then the combination fg means 'put the result of g into the f formula'.

Trying this with $x = 2$, $g(2) = 2 + 2 = 4$. Now put 4 into the f formula: $f(4) = 4^2 - 4(4) = 16 - 16 = 0$. So $fg(2) = 0$.

A formula for fg can be found:

$$fg(x) = f(g(x))$$

using flow diagrams of p. 47

$$x \rightarrow \boxed{g} \rightarrow \boxed{f} \rightarrow fg(x)$$

$$= f(x + 2)$$
$$= (x + 2)^2 - 4(x + 2)$$

where the expression $x + 2$ has been put in place of x in the formula. Simplifying:

$$fg(x) = (x + 2)(x + 2) - 4(x + 2)$$
$$= (x + 2)x + (x + 2)2 - 4x - 8$$
$$= x^2 + 2x + 2x + 4 - 4x - 8$$
$$= x^2 - 4$$

So the formula is $fg(x) = x^2 - 4$.

The functions fg and gf are quite different. Reversing the order produces a different result. The formula for $gf(x)$ is $gf(x) = x^2 - 4x + 2$ (check this).

Example *Given that* $f : x \rightarrow \frac{1}{x}$ *and* $g : x \rightarrow (x + 1)^2$ *then* $gf(2) =$
$A \frac{1}{9}$ $B 1\frac{1}{4}$ $C 2\frac{1}{4}$ $D 4\frac{1}{2}$ $E 9\frac{1}{2}$ (LON)

Answer	**Comments**
$gf(2) = g(f(2)) = g(\frac{1}{2})$	as $f(2) = \frac{1}{2}$

$$= \left(\frac{1}{2} + 1\right)^2$$

$$= \left(\frac{3}{2}\right)^2 = \frac{9}{4}$$

$= 2\frac{1}{4}$; so the answer is C.

A formula is very useful for calculating values. However, when very many values of x are given, the calculations become tedious. In this case it is better to draw a graph for a few values of x.

Graphs: Drawing and Using Them

The first step is to calculate values of the function for a few values of x. This is best laid out in the form of a table, which decreases the chances of arithmetical errors and makes it easier to check. As an example, take the function $f(x) = x^2 - 3x + 2$. This expression has three terms, x^2, $-3x$ and 2. All of them have to be worked out in the table:

x	-3	-2	-1	0	1	2	3	4
x^2	9	4	1	0	1	4	9	16
$-3x$	9	6	3	0	-3	-6	-9	-12
2	2	2	2	2	2	2	2	2
y	20	12	6	2	0	0	2	6

Notes

(i) The final value is denoted by y

(ii) Any minus signs are included in each term, so that the columns are added.

(iii) The constant number 2 keeps the same value across the table: do *not* multiply by x.

(iv) Be very careful when squaring and multiplying, especially when the numbers are negative. Do the calculations accurately since *everything else will depend on getting the table right*.

The table provides pairs of values of x and y which can now be plotted as *points* on graph paper.

Plotting the graph

When using graph paper there are some basic rules to obey:

(i) Use pencil only, even for the axes and your name. Ink could very easily smudge and make reading the graph difficult.

(ii) Place the axes so as to make best use of the paper.

(iii) You will usually be told what scale to use. Make sure you do.

(iv) Plot the points clearly with a '$\times$' cross. Use an HB pencil which has been sharpened.

(v) Join the points with a clear, smooth curve. Try to draw it as a continuous line. You get the best results if you turn the page so that you are drawing from beneath the curve. In this way you can rest your elbow on the table while drawing. If the graph is meant to be a straight line, use a ruler which is long enough.

(vi) Finally, make sure that the axes are marked and that the graph is identified by putting the formula at the top of the page.

Drawing the axes: look at the table of values and find the range of values for both the xs and the ys. In the example x goes from -3 up to 4 and y from 0 to 20. So the y-axis must be somewhere near the middle of the paper while the x-axis is at the bottom:

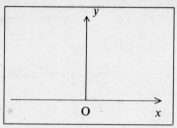

The axes meet at the *origin* O.

The *x* values are always plotted along the horizontal axis, and the *y* values along the vertical axis.

Now the scale has to be marked on each axis. In this example, take 2 cm for 1 unit on the *x*-axis and 1 cm for 4 units on the *y*-axis.

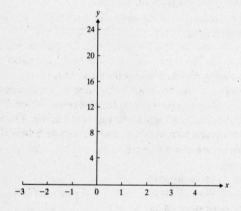

To plot the points: for each value of *x* in turn, the height above the *x*-axis is given by the corresponding value of *y*. If the *y* value is negative, then the point is below the *x*-axis.

Use an '×' type cross, rather than a '+' or . , because it shows up more clearly and is easier to draw lines through accurately.

Drawing the graph: join the × s smoothly. Remember to turn the paper so that you are always drawing from underneath the arc of the curve.

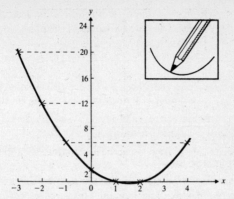

The x and y values are known as the *coordinates* of the point. They are often put in brackets: for example (3,2) is the point with x value 3 and y value 2. The x value is always the first one.

Using the graph

The graph can be used to find the value of y for a given value of x. For example, if $x = 2·5$, the point on the curve with this value of x has a height of approximately 0·8, which is the value of y.

The graph can also be used to find a value of x corresponding to a given value of y. For example if $y = 5$, draw a horizontal line at the height of 5, and find the points where this line cuts the curve. The x values of these points are the required numbers. From the graph below, these values turn out to be $x = 3·8$ and $x = -0·8$.

This corresponds to solving the equation $x^2 - 3x + 2 = 5$, since $x^2 - 3x + 2$ is y, which is set to the value 5.

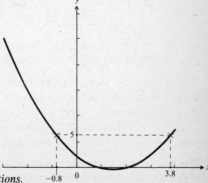

Graphs can be used to solve equations.

Two graphs drawn on the same diagram may well intersect. If the two functions are $f(x)$ and $g(x)$, then the x values of the points of intersection are solutions of the equation $f(x) = g(x)$.

For example, taking $f(x) = x^2 - 3x + 2$, the graph drawn above, and $g(x) = 2x + 1$.

It is only necessary to plot three points for the function $2x + 1$ as it is a *straight line*. Any function that only involves the first power of x, no x^2, x^3, $\sqrt{x}$, $\frac{1}{x}$ terms, is a straight line. Two of the points fix the line, and the third acts as a check for accuracy.

The x values of the points of intersection are 4·8 and 0·2. So the solutions of the equation $x^2 - 3x + 2 = 2x + 1$ are 4·8 and 0·2.

The main disadvantage of graphical methods is that they tend to have a poor accuracy. You can test the accuracy of this example by simplifying the equation to: $x_2 - 5x + 1 = 0$ and then using the formula of p. 57 to solve the equation.

Sketching graphs

When only a rough idea of the shape of the curve is required, it is not necessary to plot the graph accurately. A rough sketch is all that is needed.

To sketch a curve, first look at the highest power of x. If it is:

(i) x, then it is a straight line

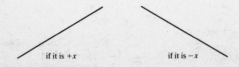

if it is $+x$ if it is $-x$

(ii) x^2, it is a quadratic

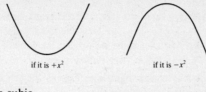

if it is $+x^2$ if it is $-x^2$

(iii) x^3, it is a cubic

if it is $+x^3$ if it is $-x^3$

Finding where the curve cuts the y-axis, the y-intercept, is done by putting $x = 0$ into the formula. Calculating one or two other points on the curve is then usually sufficient to give a good idea of the shape. For some cubics the humps can be very small, or even non-existent.

More detailed curve sketching can be found on p. 90.

Examination questions and examples

1. Functions f and g are defined on the set of real numbers by $f(x) = \frac{1}{2}x^2 + 6$ and $g(x) = 7 - x$.
  (i) Calculate $f(1\cdot5)$ and $f(-1\cdot5)$.
  (ii) Solve the equation $f(2x) = f(4x - 2)$.
  (iii) Sketch the graphs of $f(x)$ and $g(x)$ on the same axes, and state the number of values of x that satisfy the equation $f(x) = g(x)$.

Answer

(i) $f(1\cdot5) = \frac{1}{2}(1\cdot5)^2 + 6$

$\qquad = \frac{1}{2} \times 2\cdot25 + 6$

$\qquad = 1\cdot125 + 6$

$\qquad = 7\cdot125$

$f(-1\cdot5) = \frac{1}{2}(-1\cdot5)^2 + 6$

$\qquad = 7\cdot125$

Comments

put $x = 1\cdot5$ into the f formula

$(-1\cdot5)^2 = 1\cdot5^2$

(ii) $f(2x) = f(4x - 2)$
$\frac{1}{2}(2x)^2 + 6 = \frac{1}{2}(4x - 2)^2 + 6$
$\frac{1}{2}(4x^2) + 6 =$ replace x by $2x$ and $4x - 2$ in the
$\frac{1}{2}(16x^2 - 16x + 4) + 6$
$2x^2 + 6 =$ formula and expand out
$8x^2 - 8x + 2 + 6$
$0 =$
$8x^2 - 2x^2 - 8x + 2 + 6 - 6$ put all terms on one side
so $6x^2 - 8x + 2 = 0$

$3x^2 - 4x + 1 = 0$ divide by 2
$(3x - 1)(x - 1) = 0$ factorize
$3x - 1 = 0$ or $x - 1 = 0$
$x = \dfrac{1}{3}$ or $x = 1$

(iii)

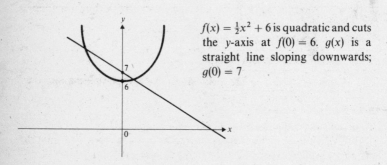

$f(x) = \frac{1}{2}x^2 + 6$ is quadratic and cuts the y-axis at $f(0) = 6$. $g(x)$ is a straight line sloping downwards; $g(0) = 7$

The graphs cut twice, and so $f(x) = g(x)$ has two solutions.

2. Copy and complete the table which gives the values of the function $y = 13 - \dfrac{12}{x}$

x	1	1·5	2·0	2·5	3·0	4·0	5·0	6·0	8·0
y	1		7·0		9·0	10·0		11·0	11·5

Using a scale of 2 cm to represent one unit on each axis, draw the graph of the curve whose equation is $y = 13 - \frac{12}{x}$ for values of x from $x = 1$ to $x = 8$.

Using the same axes and scales, draw the graph of the straight line whose equation is $y = x + 5.5$.

Write down, but do not simplify, the equation in x satisfied by the values of x at the points of intersection of the curve and the straight line. Write down, from your graphs, the solutions of this equation. (AEB)

Answer

x	1	1·5	2·0	2·5	3·0	4·0	5·0	6·0	8·0
13	13	13·0	13·0	13·0	13·0	13·0	13·0	13·0	13·0
$-\dfrac{12}{x}$	-12	$-8\cdot0$	$-6\cdot0$	$-4\cdot8$	$-4\cdot0$	$-3\cdot0$	$-2\cdot4$	$-2\cdot0$	$-1\cdot5$
y	1	5·0	7·0	8·2	9·0	10·0	10·6	11·0	11·5

See graph on p. 78.

Comments

Table for $y = x + 5.5$

x	1	3	6
5·5	5·5	5·5	5·5
y	6·5	8·5	11·5

three points for a straight line

The equation satisfied at the points of intersection is

$$13 - \frac{12}{x} = x + 5.5 \qquad\qquad f(x) = g(x)$$

From the graph, the solutions are
$x = 2.3$ and $x = 5.5$.

Notes   You should show all the construction lines on the graph showing how the solutions were arrived at. Indicate the solutions on the x-axis.

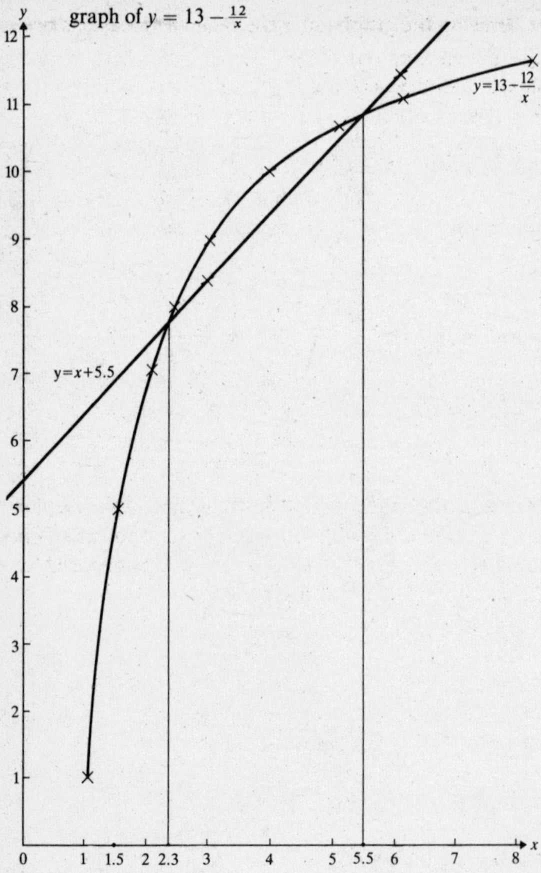

graph of $y = 13 - \frac{12}{x}$

$y = 13 - \frac{12}{x}$

$y = x + 5.5$

Graphs and Inequalities

Simple inequalities were dealt with on p. 64; more complicated ones can be solved with the help of graphs.

Example *Draw the graph of the function* $y = 7x - x^3$ *for the range of values of* x *from* -3 *to* 3, *and from your graph determine for what values of* x *in this range* $7x - x^3 > 4$ (O X F *part*)

Answer   Drawing the graph (after the table of values has been made):
(Check this by working out the table yourself, and drawing the graph on graph paper.)

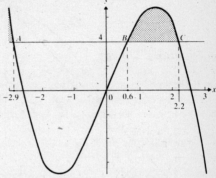

Draw a horizontal line through 4 on the *y*-axis. This line cuts the curve at A, B and C. Drop lines down to the *x*-axis from these points. When the curve is above this line, then $7x - x^3 > 4$. This happens for the values of *x* in the range $x < -2.9$ and $0.6 < x < 2.2$.

Section 7: Slopes and Gradients

How Functions Change

A graph shows how quickly the function responds to a change in the value of x. The curve below has steep parts, which respond quickly to an increase in x, and less steep parts, which respond slowly:

When x increases from 1 to 2, y increases from 1 to 2. When x increases from 5 to 6, y increases from 3 to 5. The relative size of the increase depends on the point of the curve.

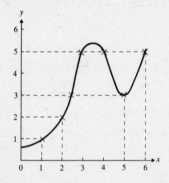

The *slope* or *gradient* of a curve at a point is the rate at which the function is increasing near that point.

For a curve, you can only consider the gradient at a particular point on the graph, since it is different at different points. There *is* one type of graph that has the same gradient at each point: the straight line

The gradient of a straight line is the same at all points on the line.

How to measure the gradient of a straight line
If you have the graph of the line, choose two points on it. They can be any two points, but for best accuracy they should be chosen far apart. Draw horizontal and vertical lines through these points to form a right-angled triangle.

The gradient of the line is $\left(\dfrac{\text{height of triangle}}{\text{base of triangle}}\right)$ and is taken as positive if the line points upwards from left to right and negative if the line points downwards.

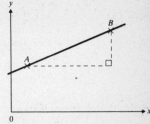

The larger the value of the gradient, the steeper the slope. If the line is vertical, then you cannot draw this triangle; the slope is infinitely large. If the line is horizontal, then the slope is zero.

Example Find the gradients of the lines

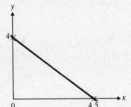 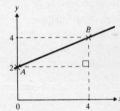

Line (i) Taking the triangle formed by the axes and the line, the height is 4, the base is 4·5, and the line slopes downwards. The gradient is $-\frac{4}{4\cdot5} = -0\cdot89$.

Line (ii) The triangle ABC has base 4, and height $4 - 2 = 2$. The line points upwards, so the gradient is positive. Gradient $= +\frac{2}{4} = \frac{1}{2}$.

Note that if a point A has coordinates x_1, y_1 and B has coordinates x_2, y_2, then the gradient of the line AB can be worked out by the formula:

$$\frac{y_2 - y_1}{x_2 - x_1}$$

How to measure the gradient of a curve
Remember that you can only find the gradient at a particular point on the curve. Choose the point where you wish to find the gradient. Draw a *tangent* at this point. This is a line which just touches the curve, without crossing it. Draw it by placing a ruler to go through the point, and then adjust the ruler until it does not cross the curve near this point (although it may cross the curve at a distant point). The gradient of the curve is

the same as the gradient of the tangent. The tangent is a straight line, so you can find its gradient by the method explained above.

Example *Find the gradient of the curve given by* $f : x \rightarrow \frac{4}{x} + \frac{x}{4}$ *at the point where* $x = 2\cdot5$ (LON part)

Answer First plot an accurate graph in the usual way. It is very important to draw the curve smoothly when you want to find the gradient. Draw a tangent at the point where $x = 2\cdot5$.

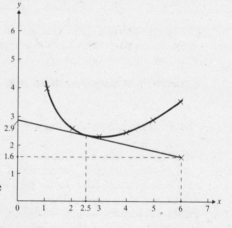

The height of the triangle is $2\cdot9 - 1\cdot6 = 1\cdot3$, and the base is 6. The line points downwards so the gradient is $-\frac{1\cdot3}{6} = -0\cdot2$.

The graph should always be drawn on graph paper, and the working should be shown on a separate piece of paper.

This way of finding the gradient depends on drawing an accurate tangent. This is quite tricky and needs practice.

Maximum and Minimum Points

These are the hilltops and valley bottoms of the graph. They are not necessarily the highest and lowest points of the whole curve, but when the range of values of x is restricted to the neighbourhood of these points, then they are the highest and lowest in that region. They should strictly be called *local* maxima and minima.

These maximum and minimum points are known as the *turning points* of the curve.

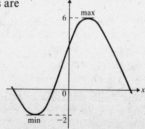

The gradient of the curve is zero at a turning point, because the tangents are horizontal.

This curve has maximum 6 and minimum -2.

It is possible to have many turning points on one curve:

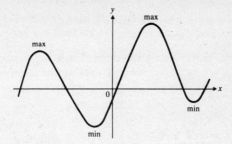

For more about turning points, see p. 88.

The Straight Line Equation y = mx + c

The most general equation for a straight line is $y = mx + c$, where m and c are constant numbers. Putting $x = 0$ in gives $y = c$. c is the value of y at the point where the line cuts the y-axis. It is the y-intercept. It turns out that m is the *gradient* of the line.

Both the gradient and the y-intercept of a line can be found from its graph, so the equation of a line can be worked out from its graph.

Example Find the equation of the straight line whose graph is:

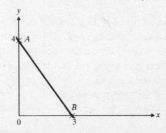

The y-intercept is 4. Taking the triangle AOB to measure the gradient, the height = 4, the base = 3 and it slopes downwards. So the gradient is $-\frac{4}{3}$.

From these measurements, $m = -\frac{4}{3}$ and $c = 4$, so the equation is $y = \frac{-4}{3}x + 4$.

This equation can be rewritten as $4x + 3y = 12$, which is another standard way of writing the equation of a straight line.

If the equation of a line is given in the form $ax + by = c$, you can find its gradient by rewriting the equation in the form $y = mx + c$.

Example Find the gradient of the line $2x - 3y = 5$

Answer $2x - 3y = 5$
Rewrite as $2x = 3y + 5$

$$3y = 2x - 5$$

$$y = \frac{2}{3}x - \frac{5}{3}$$

The gradient can be read off as $\frac{2}{3}$.

Parallel lines have the same gradient, so that the lines $y = 2x + 3$ and $y = 2x - 5$ are parallel, as they both have gradient 2.

Given two points on a line, you can find its gradient. The best way is to draw a diagram, which need not be accurate.

Example Find the gradient of the line joining the points (1,3) and (5,9).

Answer   Remember that (1,3) is the point $x = 1$ and $y = 3$, (5,9) is the point $x = 5$ and $y = 9$.

Base = 4

Height = 6

Gradient = $\frac{6}{4}$ = 1·5

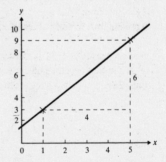

Inequalities and the plane

Inequalities can be used to specify regions of the $x - y$ plane. For example, $x \geqslant 0$ is the right-hand side of the y-axis. $1 \leqslant x \leqslant 6$ is a vertical strip, $-4 \leqslant y \leqslant 9$ is a horizontal strip.

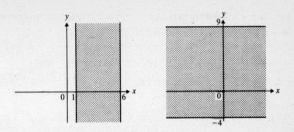

Putting the two inequalities together gives the box

$$1 \leqslant x \leqslant 6$$
$$\text{and } -4 \leqslant y \leqslant 9$$

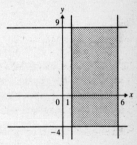

Straight lines divide the plane into two halves. The line $2x + y = 6$ divides the plane into the halves which can be represented by the inequalities $2x + y \leqslant 6$ and $2x + y \geqslant 6$. To find out which half is given by each inequality, put in the values of x and y for some of the points in the plane.

For example, $(-1,0)$ is on the left of the line, and the value of $2x + y$ is $-2 < 6$. Therefore the inequality $2x + y < 6$ is on the left side of the line. $2x + y > 6$ is on the right side.

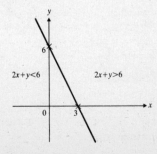

Example Calculate the area of the region defined by the inequalities $x \geqslant 0$, $y \geqslant 0$, $2x + y \leqslant 4$.

Answer   First draw the region defined by these inequalities. It is bounded by the lines $x = 0$, $y = 0$ and $2x + y = 4$.

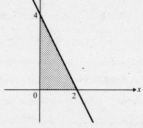

Note that $2x + y = 4$ cuts the x-axis at $x = 2$ and the y-axis at $y = 4$. The region is a triangle of height 4 and base 2, so that its area is $\frac{1}{2}$ base $\times$ height (see p. 108) $= \frac{1}{2} \times 2 \times 4 = 4$ square units.

Gradients by Calculation $\left(\frac{dy}{dx}\right)$

Graphical methods are useful but not very accurate for finding gradients of curves. Fortunately there is a method for finding gradients by calculation; it is known as *differentiation.*

The following table gives powers of x, and their corresponding gradient functions. The gradient is a function because its value changes as x changes.

function	1	x	x^2	x^3	x^4	x^5	x^6	x^n
gradient function	0	1	$2x$	$3x^2$	$4x^3$	$5x^4$	$6x^5$	nx^{n-1}

The rule is, multiply x by the power and subtract 1 from the power for the new power. The last entry in the table gives the general case, when n can be any power. Putting $n = 1, 2, 3, 4 \ldots$ gives the first few entries. (Use has been made of $x^1 = x$ and $x^0 = 1$.)

The variable x was used, but the same rule applies no matter what letters are used. For example, if $r = t^2$, then the gradient of the function r is $2t$.

To find the numerical value of the gradient, it is necessary to know the value of x to put into the gradient formula.

Examples 1. Differentiate $y = x^{10}$.

Answer Using the formula with $n = 10$, the gradient is $10x^9$.

2. Find the gradient of the function $y = x^6$ when $x = 2$.

Answer The gradient function is $6x^5$. Putting in $x = 2$, the gradient $= 6(2^5) = 6 \times 32 = 192$.

To find the gradient functions of more complicated expressions, split them up into separate powers of x, and then use the table or formula to differentiate the powers.

Example Find the gradient function of the expression

$$y = 2x^2 - 5x + 4$$

Answer Bracket the separate powers of x:

$$y = 2(x^2) - 5(x) + 4(1)$$

leaving the multiplying factors outside the brackets.
Differentiate the terms in brackets

$$2(2x) - 5(1) + 4(0)$$

which, when simplified, gives

$$4x - 5$$

which is the gradient function.

Notice that the constant term at the end becomes zero when differentiated.

$\frac{dy}{dx}$ notation

The gradient function is denoted by $\frac{dy}{dx}$, which translates as 'differentiate y with respect to x'. 'With respect to x' means that the expression is a function of the variable x. If the function involves a different letter, t say, then the gradient would be written as $\frac{dy}{dt}$.

Using this notation,

$$\text{if } y = x^n \text{ then } \frac{dy}{dx} = nx^{n-1}$$

Summary To differentiate the function of x

$$y = 2x^2 - 5x + 4$$

(i) Bracket the powers of x

$$y = 2(x^2) - 5(x) + 4(1)$$

(ii) Use the formula to differentiate each bracketed power

$$\frac{dy}{dx} = 2(2x) - 5(1) + 4(0)$$

(iii) Remove the brackets and simplify

$$\frac{dy}{dx} = 4x - 5$$

The function $y = \frac{1}{x}$

$\frac{1}{x}$ can be written as x^{-1} (see p. 32), and the formula for differentiating can then be used with $n = -1$.

$$\frac{dy}{dx} = -1(x^{-1-1}) = -x^{-2} = -\frac{1}{x^2}$$

The negative power means reciprocal.

To calculate turning points

At the turning point of a curve the gradient is zero (see p. 82). This allows us to find maximum and minimum points on a curve:

(i) Find $\frac{dy}{dx}$, the gradient function.
(ii) Set this to zero, giving an equation in x.
(iii) Solve this equation.
(iv) Put the solutions of this equation into the y *formula.*

Example *Find the maximum and minimum values of the function* $y = x^3 - 3x^2 - 9x$. (AEB part)

Answer   First differentiate the function

$$y = (x^3) - 3(x^2) - 9(x)$$

$$\frac{dy}{dx} = (3x^2) - 3(2x) - 9(1)$$

$$= 3x^2 - 6x - 9$$

Set this to zero

$$3x^2 - 6x - 9 = 0$$

$$x^2 - 2x - 3 = 0 \qquad \text{dividing by 3}$$

$$(x - 3)(x + 1) = 0 \qquad \text{factorizing}$$
$$x - 3 = 0 \text{ or } x + 1 = 0$$
$$x = 3 \text{ or } x = -1$$

Putting these values into the y formula gives the values

$$y = 3^3 - 3(3^2) - 9(3) = 27$$

and $\qquad y = (-1)^3 - 3(-1)^2 - 9(-1) = -1 - 3 + 9 = 5.$

You would expect the value 27 to be maximum, and 5 to be the minimum. This is in fact the case, but it is not always true that the maximum is greater than the minimum. The graph of $y = x + \frac{1}{x}$ shows that the maximum is the smaller of the two.

It is necessary to have a test which will show which is the maximum and which is the minimum. A test that can be used is as follows:

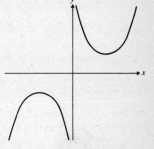

(i) Find the value of the gradient function at two points either side of the turning point.

(ii) Look at the signs of these gradients. If the signs change from $+$ to $-$ as x increases, then it is a maximum point. If the signs change from $-$ to $+$, it is a minimum point.

This is best done by making tables of values:

In the last example, $y = x^3 - 3x^2 - 9x$, the turning points were at $x = -1$ and $x = 3$. The gradient function is $\frac{dy}{dx} = 3x^2 - 6x - 9$.

x	-2	-1	0
$\dfrac{dy}{dx}$	15	0	-9
	$+$		$-$

x	2	3	4
$\dfrac{dy}{dx}$	-9	0	15
	$-$		$+$

The values of x have been put into the gradient formula. The first table shows a sign change of $+$ to $-$, representing a maximum. The second has − to +, which is a minimum. It does not matter too much what values of x near the turning values are used, but they should be close together. The gradient value in the centre is always zero.

More about Curve Sketching

Having found any maximum or minimum points on a curve, it is possible to sketch the graph more accurately. If the points where the curve meets the y-axis (y-intercepts) and the x axis (x-intercepts) are known, then it is quite easy to sketch the curve.

Example *Sketch the curve $y = 2x^2 − 6x + 5$* (A E B part)

Answer   First find the point where the curve meets the y-axis.
It meets the y-axis when $x = 0$, so $y = 5$.
Now find any turning points

$$\frac{dy}{dx} = 2(2x) − 6(1) + 5(0)$$

$$= 4x − 6$$

For a turning point $4x − 6 = 0$

$$4x = 6$$

$$x = \frac{6}{4} = \frac{3}{2} = 1 \cdot 5$$

Make a gradient table:

x	1	1·5	2
$\dfrac{dy}{dx}$	−2	0	2
	−		+

Sign changes − to + so it is a minimum.
The minimum is when $x = 1 \cdot 5$, $y = 2(1 \cdot 5)^2 − 6(1 \cdot 5) + 5$

$$= 2(2 \cdot 25) − 9 + 5$$

$$= 4 \cdot 5 − 9 + 5 = 0 \cdot 5$$

Put this in a diagram:

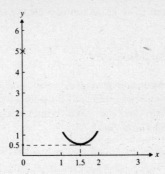

Join up this minimum point and the y-intercept with a smooth curve.

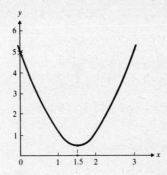

Note that the shape is what is expected for an x^2 function (p. 75). Note also that all the information about the curve was obtained by setting various quantities to 0: the y-intercept from putting $x = 0$, the minimum from putting $\frac{dy}{dx} = 0$.

Section 8: Integration: $\int \ldots dx$

Differentiating a function gives its gradient. Sometimes, particularly in the Physical Sciences, the gradient function is known and the problem is then to find the original function. This process is called integration and is the reverse of differentiation. The gradient table of p. 86 can be used backwards, by seeing which function corresponds to the given gradient function.

It is more convenient to draw up a new table where the factors have been divided out from the $\frac{dy}{dx}$ row for convenience.

$\dfrac{dy}{dx}$	0	1	x	x^2	x^3	x^4	x^5	x^n
y		1	x	$\dfrac{1}{2}x^2$	$\dfrac{1}{3}x^3$	$\dfrac{1}{4}x^4$	$\dfrac{1}{5}x^5$	$\dfrac{1}{6}x^6$	$\dfrac{1}{n+1}x^{n+1}$

The last entry is the general formula. To integrate a power of x, add 1 on to the power for the new power, and then divide x by the new power.

Example *If the gradient function is 2x, and $y = 1$ when $x = 2$, find a formula for y in terms of x.* (AEB part)

Answer $\dfrac{dy}{dx} = 2(x)$, using the table to integrate x:

$$y = 2\left(\frac{1}{2}x^2\right) = x^2$$

This is not quite the complete answer. Differentiating $x^2 + 1$, $x^2 + 2$ and so on also gives $\frac{dy}{dx} = 2x$, since any constant term becomes 0 when differentiated. We cannot say what number should be added on, so write

$$y = x^2 + c$$

where c is any constant number and is called the *constant of integration*.

The question gave more information, that $y = 1$ when $x = 2$. This information enables us to find the value of c. Put these values of x and y into the formula obtained by integrating:

$$1 = 2^2 + c$$

$$1 = 4 + c$$

$$\text{so } c = -3$$

Put this value of c back into the formula:

$$y = x^2 - 3$$

is the complete answer to the problem.

Summary Split off the powers of x; use the table or formula to integrate these powers, and put $+c$ on the end. Find c by putting in given values for x and y.

Example Integrate $x^3 - 2x^2 + 4$ with respect to x.

(Remember that 'with respect to x' just means that the formulae should have xs in them.)

Answer The gradient function is $\dfrac{dy}{dx} = x^3 - 2x^2 + 4$

$$= (x^3) - 2(x^2) + 4(1)$$

Integrate the powers $y = (\tfrac{1}{4}x^4) - 2(\tfrac{1}{3}x^3) + 4(x) + c$

Simplify $y = \tfrac{1}{4}x^4 - \tfrac{2}{3}x^3 + 4x + c$

In this example, no pair of value for x and y is given, so the value of c cannot be worked out.

The ∫ Notation

The phrase 'integrate $x^3 + 1$ with respect to x' can be put in symbols as $\int (x^3 + 1)dx$ where the $\int$ sign means integrate, and the dx is 'with respect to x'. If the formula is a function of t, for example, then a dt is used in place of the dx.

The worked example above could be written as

$$\int (x^3 - 2x^2 + 4)dx = \tfrac{1}{4}x^4 - \tfrac{2}{3}x^3 + 4x + c$$

Integration and Areas under Curves

Another use of integration is to find areas. The example on p. 90 asked for a sketch of the curve $y = 2x^2 - 6x + 5$. Now we can find the area bounded by the curve, the x-axis, the y-axis and the line $x = 3$.

The area is shaded on the diagram.

To find this area
   (i) Integrate the function
  (ii) Put $x = 3$ into the
      formula obtained
 (iii) Put $x = 0$ into this
      formula.
 (iv) Subtract the answer of
      (iii) from the answer of (ii).

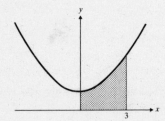

Integrating first gives

$$\int (2x^2 - 6x + 5)\mathrm{d}x = 2(\tfrac{1}{3}x^3) - 6(\tfrac{1}{2}x^2) + 5(x)$$

$$= \tfrac{2}{3}x^3 - 3x^2 + 5x$$

(When using integration to find areas, leave the c out.)

Put in $x = 3$ $\tfrac{2}{3}(3)^3 - 3(3)^2 + 5(3) = 6$

Put in $x = 0$ $\tfrac{2}{3}(0)^3 - 3(0)^2 + 5(0) = 0$

Subtracting $6 - 0 = 6$

The required area is 6 square units.

The definite integral
When working out the area, the two values of x are usually put around the integral sign, to remind you that they must be substituted into the formula. The result, $\int_0^3 (2x^2 - 6x + 5)\mathrm{d}x$, is called a *definite integral*. The larger of the two numbers is usually written at the top. They are called the *limits of the integration.*

The working is usually set out in the following way:

Example Find $\int_1^2 x^2 dx$.

Answer $\int_1^2 x^2 dx = \left[\frac{1}{3}x^3\right]_1^2 = \left(\frac{1}{3}2^3\right) - \left(\frac{1}{3}1^3\right)$

$$= \frac{8}{3} - \frac{1}{3}$$

$$= \frac{7}{3}$$

The square brackets are also to remind you to put the two values of x into the formula.

Volumes of Revolution

If part of a curve is rotated completely about the x-axis, it sweeps out the surface of a *solid of revolution*. The volume of this solid can be found from the formula

$$\text{Volume} = \pi \int_a^b y^2 dx$$

where a and b are the lowest and highest values of x (see figure below).

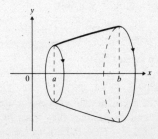

Examples

1. A curve has gradient function $2x - 7$ and passes through the point $(-1, 7)$. Find the equation of this curve.

Answer	**Comments**
$\dfrac{\mathrm{d}y}{\mathrm{d}x} = 2x - 7$	gradient function
$y = 2\left(\dfrac{1}{2}x^2\right) - 7(x) + c$	integrate each term
$y = x^2 - 7x + c$	

When $x = -1, y = 7$
$$y = (-1)^2 - 7(-1) + c$$
$$7 = 1 + 7 + c$$
$$c = -1$$
$$y = x^2 - 7x - 1$$

2. (i) Sketch the graph of the function $y = x^2 + 2x - 3$.

(ii) Find the minimum value of this function.

(iii) If the curve cuts the x-axis at the points A and B and M is the minimum point, find the area of triangle AMB.

(iv) Calculate the area bounded by the line segments AM and MB and the curve.

Answer	**Comments**
(i) Put $x = 0$:	find where the curve cuts the y-axis
$\qquad y = 0^2 + 2(0) - 3 = -3$	
Put $y = 0$:	find where the curve cuts the x-axis
$\qquad 0 = x^2 + 2x - 3$	
$\qquad 0 = (x + 3)(x - 1)$	factorize
$\qquad x = -3$ or $x = 1$	$x + 3 = 0$ or $x - 1 = 0$

The graph is   from general shape of x^2 curve

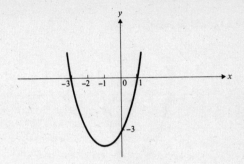

(ii) The minimum is when $\dfrac{dy}{dx} = 0$ (see p. 88)

$y = x^2 + 2x - 3$

$\dfrac{dy}{dx} = 2x + 2 = 0$

$\qquad 2x = -2$

$\qquad\quad x = -1$ x value

$y = (-1)^2 + 2(-1) - 3$ find y value

$\quad = 1 - 2 - 3$

$y = -4.$

The minimum value is -4.

(iii)

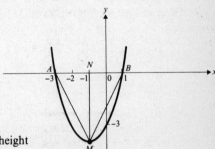

Area of $\triangle ABM = \frac{1}{2}$base $\times$ height

$= \frac{1}{2} \times AB \times MN$

$= \frac{1}{2} \times 4 \times 4$ $MN = y$ coordinate of M

$= 8$

The triangle has area 8 square units

(iv)

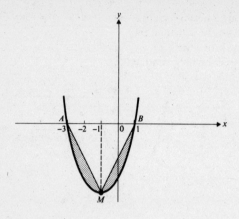

First find the area between the curve and the x-axis by integration.

$$\int_{-3}^{1} y\,dx = \int_{-3}^{1} (x^2 + 2x - 3)\,dx \qquad x \text{ limits are } -3 \text{ at } A \text{ and } 1 \text{ at } B$$

$$= \left[\left(\frac{1}{3}x^3 \right) + (x^2) - 3(x) \right]_{-3}^{1}$$

$$= \left(\frac{1}{3}(1)^3 + (1)^2 - 3(1) \right)$$

$$- \left(\frac{1}{3}(-3)^3 + (-3)^2 - 3(-3) \right) \qquad \text{substituting limits}$$

$$= \left(\frac{1}{3} + 1 - 3 \right) - \left(\frac{1}{3} \times 27 + 9 + 9 \right)$$

$$= \left(\frac{1}{3} - 2 \right) - (9 + 9 + 9)$$

$$= \left(\frac{1 - 6}{3} \right) - 27$$

$$= -\frac{5}{3} - 27 \qquad \text{work carefully here!}$$

$$= \frac{-5 - 81}{3} = -\frac{86}{3}$$

Since the area must be positive, the area between the curve and the axis is $\frac{86}{3}$ square units. The shaded area is found by subtracting the area of the triangle

$$\frac{86}{3} - 8 = \frac{86 - 24}{3} = \frac{62}{3}$$

the required area is $20\frac{2}{3}$ square units.   as a mixed number

Section 9: Speed, Distance and Time

The average speed of a moving object is given by the formula

$$\text{speed} = \frac{\text{distance travelled}}{\text{time taken}}$$

This formula can be rearranged, to give

$$\text{time taken} = \frac{\text{distance travelled}}{\text{speed}}$$

and

$$\text{distance} = \text{speed} \times \text{time}$$

When the speed is constant, then the formula gives the actual speed, which is the same as the average speed.

Example *A motorcyclist plans to visit a friend who lives 50 km away. He estimates that his average speed for the journey will be 50 km/h. Assuming that his average speed could be 10 km/h greater or smaller than his estimate, calculate, in minutes, the difference between his earliest and latest times of arrival.* (AEB)

Answer The smallest value for the average speed is 40 km/h, and the greatest is 60 km/h. Use the second formula for calculating the time taken:

$$\text{At a speed of 40 km/h} \qquad \text{time} = \frac{50}{40} = 1\tfrac{1}{4} \text{ hours}$$

$$\text{At a speed of 60 km/h} \qquad \text{time} = \frac{50}{60} = \frac{5}{6} \text{ hours.}$$

Convert the times into minutes by multiplying by 60:

Longest time $\quad = 1\tfrac{1}{4} \times 60 = 75$ minutes

Shortest time $\quad = \dfrac{5}{6} \times 60 = 50$ minutes

Difference $\quad = 25$ minutes.

Distance–Time Graphs

The distance from a fixed point, O, is plotted against time. A typical distance–time graph looks like this:

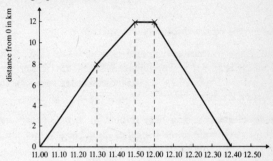

time in hours and minutes

The graph, which consists of straight-line segments, represents the distance of a cyclist from his starting point (O) plotted against time.

Examination question

Find the average speeds, in km/h, of the cyclist: (i) between 11.00 and 11.30; (ii) on his outward journey; (iii) on his return journey.

At 11.30 a pedestrian was 12 km from O and walked towards O at a steady speed of 6 km/h. Plot the straight-line graph of his path, and hence find the times on the two occasions when he met the cyclist. (OXF)

Answer

The average speed is given by the formula $\frac{\text{distance}}{\text{time}}$. For a straight-line segment of the graph, this is just the gradient.

(i) The line segment for the journey between 11.00 and 11.30 has height 8 and base 0.5 (in hours, remember that 30 mins = $\frac{1}{2}$ h). The gradient of this segment is $\frac{8}{0.5} = 16$. The speed for this part of the journey is 16 km/h.

(ii) The distance is increasing until time 11.50; at this time the gradient becomes zero because the cyclist stops. At 12.00 he starts off again, but the line slopes downwards, the distance is decreasing, so that this is the return part of the journey. His outward journey is between 11.00 and 11.50, a total time of 50 minutes. The distance travelled is 12 km, so that the average speed is $12 \div \frac{50}{60}$. The time has been converted from minutes to hours by dividing by 60.

$$\text{speed} = 12 \div \frac{50}{60}$$

$$= 12 \times \frac{60}{50} = 14{\cdot}4 \text{ km/h}$$

The speed for the outward journey was 14·4 km/h.

(iii) The return journey takes place from 12.00 to 12.40, a time of 40 minutes, which is $\frac{40}{60} = \frac{2}{3}$ h. The distance travelled is 12 km, so that the average speed is $12 \div \frac{2}{3} = 12 \times \frac{3}{2} = 18$. The average speed for the return journey was 18 km/h.

In this kind of question it is very important to make sure that all the quantities are in the right units. The times should be in hours, the distances in km, and the speeds in km/h.

For the last part of the question, the line representing the walker's journey must be added to the diagram. He starts at 11.30 at a distance of 12 km from O. The starting point of the line is then at a height of 12 above the 11.30 mark on the time-axis.

After an hour, travelling at 6 km/h, he has walked 6 km and is now a distance of 6 km from O. This gives a point at height 6 above the 12.30 mark. These two points allow us to draw the line.

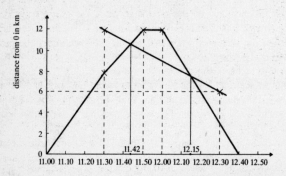

The walker and the cyclist meet at 11.42 and 12.15, the times for which the journey lines cross.

Speed–Time Graphs

These can also be plotted, with the speed on the vertical axis. On the distance–time graph, the speed is given by the gradient of the line. A gradient corresponds to differentiating. The reverse of differentiating is integration, which corresponds to the area under a graph (see p. 94). *The area under a speed–time graph represents the distance travelled.*

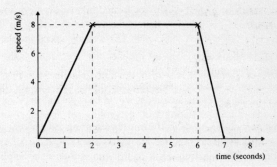

Example *Find the total distance travelled in 7 seconds, from this speed–time graph.* (LON)

Answer
The journey breaks up into three parts. From 0 to 2 seconds the speed is steadily increasing. For the next 4 seconds the speed stays constant at 8 m/s (which is sometimes written as 8 m s^{-1}), and then decreases to zero over the next second. Working out the area under the graph for each stage of the journey:

For the first 2 seconds   Area of triangle = $\frac{1}{2}$ × base × height (see p. 108)
$$= \tfrac{1}{2} \times 2 \times 8 = 8$$

For the next 4 seconds   Area of rectangle = base × height (see p. 110)
$$= 4 \times 8 = 32$$

For the last second   Area of triangle = $\frac{1}{2}$ × base × height
$$= \tfrac{1}{2} \times 1 \times 8 = 4$$

Adding these distances gives 44.
The total distance travelled was **44 metres**.

The gradient of a speed–time graph also has a meaning: it is the acceleration. The acceleration tells you how the speed is changing. If the acceleration is positive, then the speed is increasing. If the acceleration is negative (a *deceleration*) then the speed is decreasing. Acceleration is measured in m/s^2 (or m s^{-2}).

Speed, Distance and Acceleration by Differentiation and Integration

The examples above depended on the fact that the graphs split up into straight-line segments, so that the gradients and areas could be easily calculated. If the speed were constantly changing, then the graphs would be curves, and the gradients and areas would be more difficult to measure. The methods of differentiating and integrating for gradients and areas (see pp. 86–94) can be used instead. If s represents distance or position, v represents the velocity (speed) and a the acceleration, then the following diagram shows the connection between them:

diff diff
$s \rightleftarrows v \rightleftarrows a$ Differentiate s to get v
int int   Differentiate v to get a
                  Integrate to get back to v and s

s, v and a are all functions of the time, t. Given one of these three functions, the other two can be found by differentiating and integrating.

Examination questions and examples

1. A particle moves along a straight line so that the velocity in m/s, after t seconds, is given by $v = 6t^2 + t - 3$.
(i) Find the distance travelled in the first two seconds.
(ii) Find the acceleration after two seconds.

Answer

(i) The velocity, v, is given. The diagram above shows that the position (s) can be found by integrating the velocity formula.

$$v = 6(t^2) + t - 3$$

Integrate $s = 6\left(\frac{t^3}{3}\right) + \frac{1}{2}t^2 - 3t + c$

using the integration rules of p. 92, *with respect to t.*

Simplify $$s = 2t^3 + \frac{1}{2}t^2 - 3t + c.$$

The position when $t = 0$ is $s = c$; the position when $t = 2$ is

$$s = 2(2^3) + \frac{1}{2}(2^2) - 3(2) + c$$

$$= 2 \times 8 + \frac{1}{2} \times 4 - 6 + c$$

$$= 16 + 2 - 6 + c$$

$$= 12 + c$$

The difference between these values is 12, and so the distance travelled in two seconds is 12 m.

(ii) To find the acceleration (a), the velocity formula must be differentiated with respect to t:

$a = 6(2t) + 1$
$a = 12t + 1$ see p. 86
When $t = 2$
$a = 12 \times 2 + 1$
$a = 24 + 1$
$a = 25$

The acceleration after two seconds is 25 m/s^2.

The constant of integration, c, gives the position of the particle when $t = 0$, called the *initial position*. We did not need to know the value of c in order to calculate the distance travelled.

The letter x is also used to denote distance, and when the distance is measured vertically upwards, the letter h is used in place of s.

2. *A ball was thrown vertically upwards and (after t seconds) its height (h metres) above the ground was given by $h = 33 + 4t - 5t^2$*

(a) *Calculate the height from which the ball was thrown.*
(b) *Find the speed with which it was thrown.*
(c) *Find the time when the speed became zero.*
(d) *Calculate the greatest height above the ground reached by the ball.*
(e) *Find how many seconds elapsed from the time the ball was thrown until it reached ground level.* (LON)

Answer

(a) When the ball was thrown

$$t = 0$$
$$h = 33 + 0 - 0$$
$$= 33$$

The ball was thrown from a height of 33 m.

(b) Differentiate to find the speed

$$h = 33(1) + 4(t) - 5(t^2)$$
$$v = 33(0) + 4(1) - 5(2t)$$
$$v = 4 - 10t$$

At the start, $t = 0$

$$v = 4 - 10(0) = 4$$

The ball was thrown with speed 4 m/s.

(c) When the speed was zero

$$4 - 10t = 0$$
$$t = \frac{4}{10} = 0.4$$

The speed was zero at 0·4 seconds.

(d) The greatest height was reached when the velocity became zero. This happened at $t = 0.4$

Comments

put $t = 0$ into h formula

express the answer in words, and state all the units used

split off the powers

differentiate

simplify

put $t = 0$ into v formula

set v formula to 0

solve the equation for t

h is max when $v = \dfrac{\mathrm{d}h}{\mathrm{d}t} = 0$

(see p. 88)

$h = 33 + 4(0.4) - 5(0.4^2)$ put $t = 0.4$ into h formula
$= 33 + 1.6 - 0.8$

$= 33.8$

The greatest height reached was 33.8 metres.

(e) The ball reached the ground
   when the height became zero

$$33 + 4t - 5t^2 = 0$$ set h to 0

$$(3 - t)(11 + 5t) = 0$$ factorize

$t = 3$ or $t = -\dfrac{11}{5}$ solve for t

The time should be positive, so
$t = 3$.
The ball reached the ground after
3 seconds.

Section 10: Shapes and Sizes

Triangles

These are three-sided figures. Their points are called vertices. Taking one of the sides as the *base* of the triangle, then the distance from the base to the opposite vertex is the height of the triangle. The height and the base must be measured at right angles to each other. The area of the triangle is given by the formula Area $= \frac{1}{2} \times$ base $\times$ height.

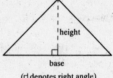

base

($\lrcorner$ denotes right angle)

The *perimeter* of a figure is the sum of the lengths of the sides. It is the distance all the way round the figure. If the sides of the triangle are denoted by the letters a, b and c, as in the diagram, then

area $= \frac{1}{2}bh$ perimeter $= a + b + c$

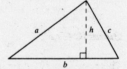

Another formula for the area of the triangle, which is useful when the height is not known, is Area $= \sqrt{s(s-a)(s-b)(s-c)}$ where $s = \frac{1}{2}(a+b+c)$, half the perimeter.

Right-angled triangles are easier to deal with, since the height is then one of the sides of the triangle. It is also possible to use *Pythagoras' Theorem* in a right-angled triangle, for calculating the lengths of sides.

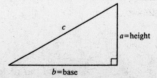

The side opposite the right angle is called the *hypotenuse* of the triangle. In words, the theorem states that *the square of the hypotenuse is equal to the sum of the squares of the other two sides*. In symbols, $c^2 = a^2 + b^2$.

Examples

(i) Find the length of the side a in this triangle.

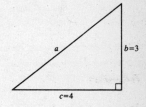

Answer $b = 3, c = 4$ so
$$a^2 = 3^2 + 4^2 = 9 + 16 = 25$$
$$a^2 = 25$$
Taking square roots, $a = 5$.

(ii) Find the length of the side b in this triangle.

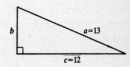

Answer $a = 13, c = 12$ so
$$13^2 = b^2 + 12^2$$
$$169 = b^2 + 144$$
$$25 = b^2 \text{ so } b = 5.$$

Pythagoras' Theorem can also be used backwards. If the sides a, b and c of a triangle satisfy the relation $a^2 = b^2 + c^2$, then the triangle has a right angle. So the triangles with sides of 3, 4 and 5 units, and of 5, 12 and 13 units, are right angled.

Quadrilaterals

These are four-sided figures. They can be cut up into two triangles whose areas can be worked out as above. The area of the quadrilateral is the sum of the areas of the separate triangles.

If the opposite sides of the quadrilateral are parallel then the figure is called a *parallelogram*, and can be split into two equal triangles. Each of the triangles has area $\frac{1}{2} \times$ base $\times$ height, so that the total area is

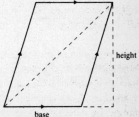

area of parallelogram = base × height.

If all the angles are right angles, then the figure is a *rectangle*; the area is given by base × height.

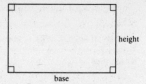

The height of the rectangle is the length of one of the sides.

Compound figures can be formed by putting triangles and quadrilaterals together. Their areas can be found by adding up all the areas of the component triangles.

A rectangle which has equal sides is called a *square*. If the sides are all of length x, then the area is x^2 and the perimeter is $4x$.

Examination question

A rectangular block of metal has a square base. The sides of the base are each x cm long and the height of the block is y cm. The sum of the lengths of the twelve edges of the block is 132 cm.

(a) Write down, in terms of x and y, an expression for A, the surface area of the block.

(b) Obtain a formula for y in terms of x, and hence prove that $A = 132x - 6x^2$.

(c) Prove that, as x varies, the greatest possible value of A is 726, and state the dimensions of the block in this case. (A E B)

Answer	Comments
(a)	always draw diagrams

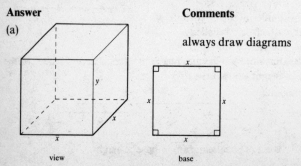

view   base

The surface of the block is made
up of:
Top with area x^2 cm^2 using area = base × height
Base of area x^2 cm^2
4 sides each of area xy cm^2
Total surface area $= 2x^2 + 4xy$

$$A = 2x^2 + 4xy$$

(b) The lengths of the 12 edges are

for the base $x, x, x, x,$
for the top $x, x, x, x,$
for the uprights $y, y, y, y.$

The total of these is $8x + 4y$

so $8x + 4y = 132$ the sum of the lengths is given
        $4y = 132 - 8x$ as 132 cm
         $y = 33 - 2x$ dividing by 4

Substitute for y in the formula for A

$$A = 2x^2 + 4x(33 - 2x)$$
$$A = 2x^2 + 132x - 8x^2$$
$$A = 132x - 6x^2$$

(c) For the greatest area, $\frac{\mathrm{d}A}{\mathrm{d}x} = 0$ see p. 88

$$\frac{\mathrm{d}A}{\mathrm{d}x} = 132 - 12x$$ differentiating

So $132 - 12x = 0$ setting to zero
     $132 = 12x$
       $x = \frac{132}{12} = 11$

Put this value into the A formula

$$A = 132(11) - 6(11^2)$$
$$= 1\,452 - 726$$
$$= 726$$

The greatest area is 726 cm^2, which happens when the sides of the
block are $x = 11$, $y = 33 - 22 = 11$ cm.

Check for maximum:

x	10	11	12	
$\dfrac{\mathrm{d}A}{\mathrm{d}x}$	+	0	−	(see p. 89)
		maximum		

Circles and arcs

The size of a circle is specified by its *radius*, the distance from the centre to the edge. If the radius is denoted by the letter r, then the area of the circle is given by the formula

$$\text{area of circle} = \pi r^2$$

where π is a constant number. It has the value 3·1416 to 4 decimal places. The fraction $\frac{22}{7}$ is a good approximation which is often used.

The perimeter of a circle is called its *circumference.* The length of the circumference is given by the formula

$$\text{circumference} = 2\pi r$$

The *diameter* of a circle is the width of the circle, measuring through the centre. It is twice the length of the radius. If the diameter of a circle is given, make sure that you remember to divide by two to get the radius to put into the above formulae.

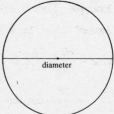

An *arc* is a piece of the perimeter of a circle. Joining its ends to the centre of the circle with two radii forms a *secto.*. The sector encloses an angle, which is usually measured in degrees. There are 360 degrees in a complete circle; a semicircle has 180 degrees, and so on:

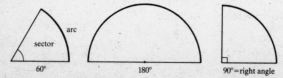

If the angle in a sector is denoted by the letter θ, then the area of the sector is given by the formula

$$\text{area of sector} = \frac{\theta}{360}\pi r^2$$

The length of the arc of the sector is

$$\text{length of arc} = \frac{\theta}{180}\pi r$$

Notice that both the area and arc length are proportional to the angle.

Example *PQR is a sector of a circle, centre P radius 7 cm. Taking $\pi = 3\frac{1}{7}$, find the length, in cm, of the arc QR.* (LON)

Answer

Angle $= \theta = 60°$, r $= 7$, so the
arc length is $\frac{60}{180} \times \frac{22}{7} \times 7$
(since $3\frac{1}{7} = \frac{22}{7}$)
$= \frac{22}{3} = 7\frac{1}{3}$ cm.

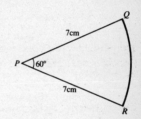

Example Find the area of the sector in the last example.

Answer Using the formula for the area of a sector

$$\text{area} = \frac{60}{360} \times \frac{22}{7} \times 7^2$$

$$= \frac{154}{6} = 25\frac{2}{3} \text{ cm}^2$$

A *segment* of a circle is that part of it cut off by a line which crosses the circle. To find its area, draw in the radii to form a sector. The area of this sector and the area of the triangle can then be calculated. The area of the segment is the difference between these two areas.

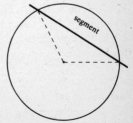

Example   Find the area of the segment shown:

Answer   The angle is a right angle which makes the calculations easier.

Area of sector $= \dfrac{90}{360} \times \dfrac{22}{7} \times 2^2 = \dfrac{22}{7}$ cm^2

Area of the right-angled triangle $= \dfrac{1}{2} \times 2 \times 2$

$$= 2 \text{ cm}^2$$

The difference of these two areas is $\dfrac{22}{7} - 2$ cm^2

$$= \dfrac{22 - 14}{7} \text{ cm}^2$$

$$= \dfrac{8}{7} \text{ cm}^2$$

$$= 1\tfrac{1}{7} \text{ cm}^2$$

Volumes

A *prism* is a shape that has a constant cross-section: no matter where you cut it across, the shape is the same:

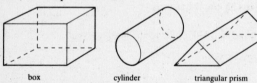

box   cylinder   triangular prism

The volume of a prism is given by

$$\text{Volume} = \text{area of cross-section} \times \text{length}$$

If the shape slopes to a point:

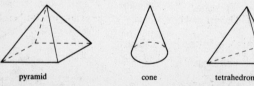

pyramid   cone   tetrahedron

then the volume is given by

$$\text{Volume of pointed shape} = \tfrac{1}{3} \times \text{base area} \times \text{height}$$

Examination question

During a storm, the depth of the rainfall was 15·4 mm. The rain which fell on a horizontal roof measuring 7·5 m by 3·6 m was collected in a cylindrical tank of radius 35 cm which was empty before the storm began. Calculate

    (a) The area in cm² of the roof

    (b) The volume in cm³ of the rain which fell on the roof.

Taking π as $\frac{22}{7}$, find

    (c) The area in cm² of the cross-section of the tank

    (d) The height in cm of the rain water in the tank.

Given that a watering-can holds five litres, how many times could it be filled completely from the rain water? (LON)

Answer

Comments

  (a) Area of roof = 750 × 360 cm²

                   = 270 000 cm²

    converting lengths to cm

  (b) Volume of rainwater

     = cross section × depth

     = 270 000 × 1·54 cm³

    converting depth into cm

     = 415 800 cm³

  (c) The cross-section of the tank is a circle of radius 35 cm; it has area

$$\pi r^2 = \frac{22}{7} \times (35^2) \text{ cm}^2$$

$$= \frac{22 \times 1225}{7} \text{ cm}^2$$

$$= 3\,850 \text{ cm}^2$$

  (d) Volume = cross section × height

     415 800 = 3 850 × height

    putting in volume and area figures

$$\text{height} = \frac{415\,800}{3\,850} \text{ cm} = 108 \text{ cm}$$

    rearranging for height

  (e) The can holds 5 litres = 5 000 cm³. The number of times it can be filled is

$$\frac{415\,800}{5\,000} = 83·16 \text{ times}$$

The can can be filled completely 83 times.

Note: It was very important to match up the units for each calculation. To convert metres to cm, multiply by 100. For cm to mm multiply by 10.

Surface area of a cone

The formula for this area is

$$\pi r l$$

where r = radius of base and l is the slant height; l can be calculated using Pythagoras' Theorem if r and h are known.

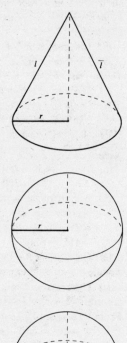

The sphere

The volume of a sphere is

$$\text{Volume} = \tfrac{4}{3}\pi r^3$$

The surface area is given by

$$\text{Area} = 4\pi r^2$$

A *hemisphere* is half of a sphere. Dividing the above formulae by two gives the volume and curved surface area of a hemisphere.

Examination question

A solid consists of a cone and a hemisphere which have a common base of diameter 20 cm. The perpendicular height of the cone is 24 cm. The figure represents the cross-section ABCD through the vertical axis AC of the solid. Calculate

(a) *The slant height of the cone*

(b) *The area, correct to the nearest cm², of the cross-section ABCD*

(c) *The total volume, correct to the nearest 10 cm³, of the solid*

(d) *The total curved surface area, correct to the nearest 10 cm², of the solid.* (AEB)

(Take π to be 3·142)

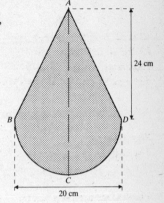

Answer

(a) The cross-section of the cone is made from two right-angled triangles. From Pythagoras' Theorem

$$l^2 = 24^2 + 10^2 = 576 + 100$$
$$= 676 \text{ cm}$$

Take the square root

$$l = 26 \text{ cm}$$

Comments

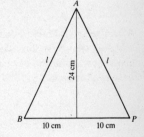

(b) Area of triangular section

$$= \tfrac{1}{2} \times 20 \times 24$$
$$= 240 \text{ cm}^2$$

area $= \tfrac{1}{2} \times$ base $\times$ height

Area of semicircle

$$= \tfrac{1}{2} \times 3 \cdot 142 \times 10^2$$
$$= 157 \text{ cm}^2 \text{ to nearest cm}^2.$$

$\tfrac{1}{2} \times \pi r^2$

So the total area is 397 cm².

add areas of two parts

(c) Volume of cone
   $= \frac{1}{3} \times 3{\cdot}142 \times 10^2 \times 24$ $\frac{1}{3} \times$ base area $\times$ height
   $= 2\,514 \text{ cm}^3$
   Volume of hemisphere
   $= \frac{2}{3} \times 3{\cdot}142 \times 10^3$ $\frac{2}{3}\pi r^3$
   $= 2\,095 \text{ cm}^3$
   Total volume   add areas of two parts and
   $= 4\,610 \text{ cm}^3.$ give answer to required
   accuracy

(d) Surface area of cone
   $= 3{\cdot}142 \times 10 \times 26$ $\pi r l$
   $= 817 \text{ cm}^2$
   Curved surface area of hemisphere
   $= 2 \times 3{\cdot}142 \times 10^2$ $2\pi r^2$
   $= 628 \text{ cm}^2$
   Total surface area
   $= 1\,450 \text{ cm}^2.$ to the required accuracy

Section 11:
Lines, Angles and Figures

Two lines which meet form an angle. If the angle is less than 90° then it is said to be acute. If the angle is greater than 90° it is obtuse. Two lines that cannot meet are said to be *parallel*.

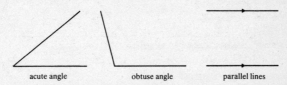

acute angle   obtuse angle   parallel lines

Parallel lines are denoted in diagrams by putting arrows on them. Equal angles are shown on diagrams by marking them with the same arc, or other symbol. For example, the angles opposite each other when two lines cross over are equal; they are called *vertically opposite angles*.

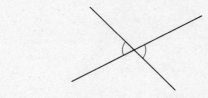

Angle properties of parallel lines:

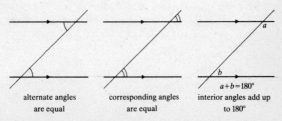

alternate angles   corresponding angles   interior angles add up
are equal   are equal   to 180°

$a+b=180°$

To show that two lines are parallel, it is enough to show that one of these properties holds.

Triangles

These are formed when three non-parallel lines cross. If all the angles are acute, then the triangle is said to be *acute angled*. The angles inside a triangle are called the interior angles. A triangle also has exterior angles which its sides form when they are lengthened.

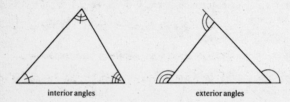

interior angles   exterior angles

Angle properties of triangles:
   (i)   The interior angles of a triangle $(x + y + z)$ add up to $180°$.
   (ii) Exterior angle = sum of opposite
         interior angles

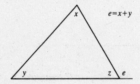

Standard notation for a triangle:
The vertices are denoted by capital letters. The side opposite the vertex A is denoted by a, the side opposite B by b, and so on. The longest side is opposite the largest angle, and the shortest side is opposite the smallest angle.

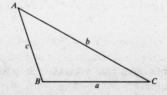

If two triangles have the same sides and angles, so that they have the same shape and size, then they are said to be *congruent*. To show that two triangles are congruent, it is not necessary to show that all the sides and angles match up. It is enough to show that

(i)   The sides of one of the triangles are the same as the sides of the other   (SSS); or

(ii) Two sides and the angle that they form are the same in both triangles   (SAS); or

(iii) Two angles and the side between them are the same in both triangles   (ASA)

The letters in brackets are mnemonics to help you remember.

Example Show that the diagonal of a parallelogram divides it into two congruent triangles.

Answer Draw the parallelogram, with the letters in cyclic order. AC is the diagonal.

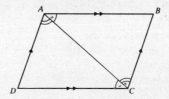

Sides AB and DC are parallel, so the angles BAC and DCA are equal (alternate angles). Also, as AD and BC are parallel, the angles BCA and DAC are equal. The side AC is in both triangles, so that the triangles have two angles and the included side equal (ASA). This shows that the triangles are congruent. We can write this as $\triangle ABC \equiv \triangle CDA$. Notice that angle A = angle C, angle B = angle D, and angle C = angle A, when the letters are written in this order.

Angle BAC means the angle formed by the lines BA and AC, and so on for the other angles. The angle ABC is often denoted by $\angle ABC$ or $A\hat{B}C$.

When writing out a geometric proof, it is important to justify all your statements by referring to particular lines and angles, and to standard properties of parallel lines and triangles. The proof should also read clearly, in good English.

Types of triangle

As earlier mentioned, an *acute-angled triangle* is one in which all the angles are less than 90°. An *obtuse-angled triangle* has one angle greater than 90° in it.

If two of the sides of a triangle are equal, then it is *isosceles*. If the three sides are all equal, then the triangle is *equilateral*. All equilateral triangles are therefore isosceles.

If you join the top vertex of an isoceles triangle to the middle of its base, it is cut into two triangles.

It is not difficult to show that the two triangles are congruent, since all the sides of one are equal to all the sides of the other triangle. This also means that the *base angles are equal*, which is a useful property of isosceles triangles.

For an equilateral triangle, all the angles are equal and since they add up to 180° they must all be 60°.

The line joining a vertex to the opposite side in a triangle, so as to form a right angle, is called an *altitude* of the triangle.

The line joining a vertex to the middle of the opposite side is called a *median*.

Notice that if two triangles have the same base and also have the same altitude then they have the same area (altitude = height).

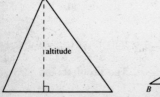

Two shapes are said to be *similar* if they have the same shape, but not necessarily the same size. For example, when you look at something through a telescope, you see an image which is similar to the object, but not the same, true size.

Two triangles are similar if they have the same angles. Since the angles of a triangle add up to 180°, it is enough to show that two angles in the two triangles are the same; the third ones will then automatically be the same.

If two triangles are similar, then all their sides are in the same ratio, for example:

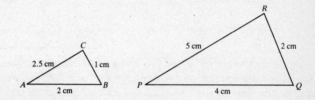

The smaller triangle has sides which are half the length of the sides of the larger triangle.

For two similar triangles ABC and PQR, where $\angle A = \angle P$, $\angle B = \angle Q$ and $\angle C = \angle R$, then this ratio property can be expressed as

$$\frac{AB}{PQ} = \frac{AC}{PR} = \frac{BC}{QR}$$

A good way to remember this is to write the letters of the two triangles one above the other, with the equal angles paired.

$$\begin{array}{l} ABC \\ PQR \end{array} \quad (\triangle ABC \text{ similar to } \triangle PQR)$$

By covering up each pair, $\frac{A}{P}$, $\frac{B}{Q}$ and $\frac{C}{R}$, in turn, the three ratios are obtained.

The converse of this is true: if two triangles have sides that satisfy the ratio property, then the two triangles are similar. Also if two sides are in the same ratio and the included angles are equal, then the triangles are similar (AAA, SSS or SAS).

Areas of Similar Shapes

For convenience, take two squares (which are automatically similar, since all the angles are 90°). Let one of the squares have a side of 1 cm, and the other have a side of 2 cm. The ratio of the sides is 1 : 2. The areas are 1 cm^2 and 4 cm^2, so that the ratio of the areas is 1 : 4.

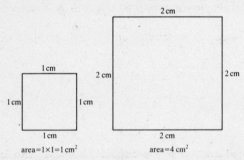

In general, *if the sides of any two similar figures are in the ratio l : m, then the areas are in the ratio l^2 : m^2.*

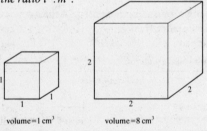

Volumes of Similar Solids

The corresponding result for volumes is that the ratio of the volumes is $l^3 : m^3$.

Quadrilaterals are four-sided figures. Rectangles, squares and parallelograms have already been met. Other types are

Trapezium One pair of sides is parallel

area = $\frac{1}{2}(a + b)h$

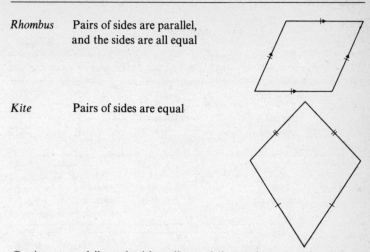

Rhombus   Pairs of sides are parallel,
and the sides are all equal

Kite   Pairs of sides are equal

Cutting a quadrilateral with a diagonal line makes two triangles, the angles of each of which add up to 180°. So *the interior angles of a quadrilateral add up to 360°*.

Each quadrilateral is distinguished by the properties of its diagonals. These are summarized in the following table, and are enough to identify each one uniquely:

Diagonal properties of quadrilaterals

shape	diagonals				diagram
	cut at 90°	bisect each other	bisect angles	equal length	
kite*	YES	ONE DOES	ONE DOES	NO (unless a rhombus)	
trapezium	POSSIBLY	NO (unless a parallelogram)	NO	POSSIBLY	
square	YES	YES	YES	YES	

shape	diagonals				diagram
	cut at 90°	bisect each other	bisect angles	equal length	
rectangle	NO (unless a square)	YES	NO (unless a square)	YES	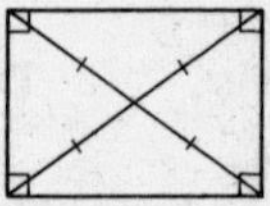
parallelo-gram	NO (unless a rhombus)	YES	NO (unless a rhombus)	NO (unless a square)	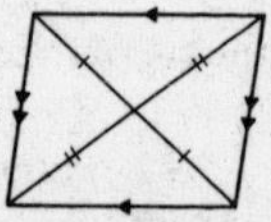
rhombus	YES	YES	YES	NO	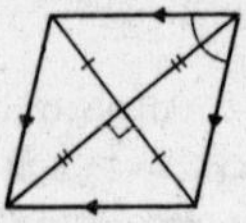

* For the kite, the long diagonal bisects the short one, and the top and bottom angles are bisected.

Other Shapes: Polygons

A polygon is the general name for shapes with many sides. Some in particular are

Pentagon   with 5 sides
Hexagon   with 6 sides
Heptagon   with 7 sides
Octagon   with 8 sides
Nonagon   with 9 sides
Decagon   with 10 sides

If all the sides of a polygon are equal, it is called a *regular polygon*, and its angles are also equal.

If all the angles are less than 180°, then the polygon is *convex* and does not turn in on itself.

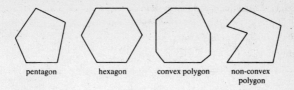

pentagon   hexagon   convex polygon   non-convex polygon

Angles of polygons

The exterior angles of any polygon add up to $360°$. The total of the interior angles depends on the number of sides. Since

the interior angle $= 180° -$ exterior angle then

the sum of the interior angles $= n180° -$ sum of exterior angles

$$= n180° - 360°$$

So, sum of interior angles $= 180°(n - 2)$.

Another way of calculating the sum of the interior angles is to draw a sketch of the polygon and cut it up into triangles. Each triangle has $180°$.

In this figure, there are 6 triangles; each triangle contributes $180°$, so that the total is $6 \times 180° = 1\,080°$.

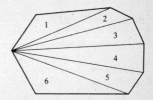

If an n-sided polygon is regular, then each interior angle is the same. In this case, each interior angle is found by dividing the total of the angles by n. Alternatively, the exterior angles can be found first:

Example Find the interior angles of a regular hexagon.

Answer The exterior angles add up to $360°$. There are 6 of them that are all equal, and so each exterior angle is $60°$. The interior angles are then $180° - 60° = 120°$.

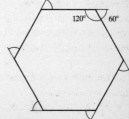

Examination questions and examples

1. The three straight lines are concurrent. Angles p, q and r are in the ratio 2:3:4. Angle p, in degrees, is
A 10° B 18° C 20° D 36° E 40°. (LON)

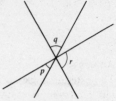

Answer

The angles
$2p + 2q + 2r = 360°$
so $p + q + r = 180°$
Dividing 180° in the ratio
$2:3:4$
$2 + 3 + 4 = 9$, $180 \div 9 = 20$
so $p = 2 \times 20° = 40°$ answer E.

Comments
concurrent means that the
lines meet at one point
the opposite angles are equal

see p. 27

2. In which one of the following four-sided figures are the diagonals ALWAYS at right angles?
A parallelogram B Quadrilateral C Rectangle D Rhombus E Trapezium
(LON)

Answer From the table on p. 125, the answer is the Rhombus, D.

3. HJKLMN is a regular hexagon. The length of the diagonal HL is 12 cm. The length in cm of HN is
A 6   B $2\sqrt{3}$ C 8   D $3\sqrt{3}$ E 9 (LON)

Answer Draw the diagonals KN and JM so that the hexagon is divided into triangles. Since the hexagon is regular, all the triangles are congruent and equilateral. So $HN = HO = \frac{1}{2}HL$. So $HN = 6$ cm, the answer is A.

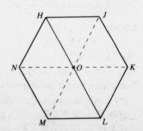

4. Given that $L\hat{X}Y = L\hat{N}M$ and $L\hat{Y}X = L\hat{M}N$ then:

A $\frac{LX}{LN} = \frac{LY}{LM}$ B $\frac{LX}{LM} = \frac{LY}{LN}$ C $\frac{LX}{XM} = \frac{LY}{YN}$

D $\frac{LX}{LM} = \frac{XY}{MN}$ E None of the above is true (LON)

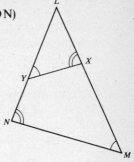

Answer $\triangle LXY$ is similar to $\triangle LNM$ (as the angles are the same)

$\frac{LXY}{LNM}$ gives $\frac{LX}{LN} = \frac{XY}{NM} = \frac{LY}{LM}$

The answer is A.

5. *The side of the square $PQRS$ is of length $m + n$, points W, X, Y and Z are taken on the sides PQ, QR, RS and SP respectively such that $PW = QX = RY = SZ = m$.*

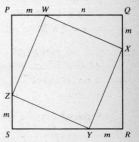

  (a) *Prove that $\triangle QXW$ is congruent to $\triangle RYX$.*

  (b) *Prove that $\angle WXY$ is a right angle.*

  (c) *Give reasons why $WXYZ$ is a square.*

  (d) *Write down, in terms of m and n, the areas of the square $PQRS$ and the triangle PWZ.*

By considering the areas of the squares and triangles, verify that $WX^2 = m^2 + n^2$.

  (e) *Given that $WY = 4m$, calculate the value of the ratio $n : m$. (LON)*

Answer   **Comments**

  (a) $\angle WQX = 90 = \angle XRY$ as
$PQRS$ is a square.

$WQ = n = RX$, and $QX = m = RY$.

The triangles are congruent (SAS).   justify the statement

  (b) Since the triangles are congruent,
$\angle QWX = \angle YXR = a°$, say, and
$\angle QXW = \angle XYR = b°$, say.

The angles of $\triangle XYR$ add up to $180°$,
so $a° + b° + 90° = 180°$.
So $a + b = 90$.
QXR is a straight line, so that

$$\angle WXY + (a° + b°) = 180°$$
$$\angle WXY = 180° - (a° + b°)$$
$$= 180° - 90° = 90°.$$

(c) $\angle WXY$ is 90, similarly $\angle XWZ$
$= \angle WZY = \angle ZYX = 90°$. Also
$WZ = ZY = YX = XW$ as all the
triangles are congruent. So $WXYZ$ is
a square.

(d) Area of square $PQRS$
$$= (m + n)^2$$
$$= m^2 + 2mn + n^2$$
Area of $\triangle PWZ = \frac{1}{2}mn$ $\frac{1}{2}$base × height
Area of square $WXYZ = WX^2$,
and $PQRS$ is made up from $WXYZ$
and 4 triangles.
Area $PQRS$ = area $WXYZ$ +
$4 \times$ area $\triangle PWZ$
$$m^2 + 2mn + n^2 = WX^2 + 4(\tfrac{1}{2}mn)$$
$$WX^2 = m^2 + n^2 + 2mn - 2mn$$
$$= m^2 + n^2$$

(e) $WY^2 = WX^2 + XY^2$ Pythagoras' Theorem
$$= 2WX^2 \text{ as } WXYZ \text{ is a}$$
square
so $(4m)^2 = 2(m^2 + n^2)$ as $WX^2 = m^2 + n^2$
$$16m^2 = 2m^2 + 2n^2$$
$$14m^2 = 2n^2$$
$$n^2 = 7m^2$$

$$\frac{n^2}{m^2} = 7$$

formula
$$\frac{n^2}{m^2} = \left(\frac{n}{m}\right)^2 = 7$$

so $n : m = \dfrac{n}{m} = \sqrt{7} : 1$

6. In the triangle ABC, the angle $\angle ACB = 60°$, DE is parallel to AB, the angle $\angle CDE = 70°$, and the angle $\angle EAB = 25°$. Calculate (a) a (b) e. (AEB)

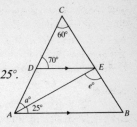

Answer

(a) DE is parallel to AB so
$$\angle CDE = \angle DAB$$
$$70° = a° + 25°$$
$$a = 45°$$

(b) $\quad e = \angle AEB$
$$= 180° - 25° - \angle ABE \text{ and}$$
$$\angle ABE = \angle DEC$$
$$= 180° - 60° - 70°$$
$$= 50°$$
so $e = 180° - 25° - 50° = 105°$.

Comments

corresponding angles

corresponding angles

7. In the figure, PQ and RS are parallel. The value of $x°$ is
A $131°$ B $137°$ C $147°$ D $151°$ (AEB)

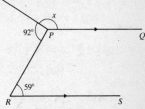

Answer

$\angle RPQ = 180° - 59° = 121°$
so $x° + 92° + 121° = 360°$
$x° = 360° - 92° - 121° = 147°$
The answer is C.

Comments
interior angles add up to 180°

8. *In the figure, the following could be true:*
I.   *WX is parallel to ZY*
II. *XY is parallel to WZ*
A I only is true   B II only is true
C Both I and II   D Neither I nor II (AEB)

Answer

(I) $72° + 108° = 180°$
So *XY* is parallel to *WZ*
Therefore II is true.

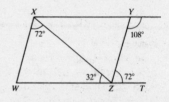

(II) $\angle XWZ = 76°$
Therefore $\angle XWT \neq \angle YZT$
So I is not true.
The answer is B.

9. Area $\triangle AXY$: Area trapezium $XYCB = 1:3$. Find AC.

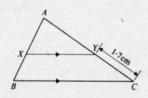

Answer	**Comments**
Triangles ABC and AXY are similar	prove this
$\dfrac{\text{Area } XYCB}{\text{Area } AXY} = \dfrac{3}{1}$ so $\dfrac{\text{Area } ABC}{\text{Area } AXY} = \dfrac{4}{1}$	ratios on p. 27
And so $\dfrac{AC}{AY} = \sqrt{\dfrac{4}{1}} = 2$	
$AC = 2 \times AY$	
$\quad\ = 2 \times YC$	if $AC = 2YC$ then $AY = YC$
$AC = 3.4$ cm	

10. *ABCD and BDEF are rectangles.*
ECF is a straight line. Prove that
   (i) *Angle ADB = angle CDE*
   (ii) *Triangles ABD, ECD and FBC*
are similar.
   (iii) *The rectangles are equal in area.*
   (iv) $\dfrac{EC}{CF} = \dfrac{(AB)^2}{(AD)^2}$ *(OXF)*

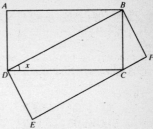

Answer

(i) Angle $ADC = 90°$, so
$\angle ADB = 90° - \angle BDC$
Also $\angle BDE = 90°$, so that
$\angle CDE = 90° - \angle BDC$. The angles
ADB and CDE are equal.

Comments

as $ABCD$ and $BDEF$ are
rectangles

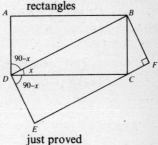

(ii) $\angle DAB = \angle DEC = 90°$ and
   $\angle ADB = \angle CDE$
So triangles ABD and ECD are
similar.
Also $\angle BFC = 90° = \angle DEC$
   $\angle BCF = 180° - 90° - \angle DCE$
      $= 90° - \angle DCE$
and $\angle CDE = 180° - 90° - \angle DCE$
so $\angle BCF = \angle CDE$, the triangles ECD
and FBC are then similar.

just proved

angles the same
$BFED$ is a rectangle
FCE is a straight line

(iii) Area of $\triangle BCD = \dfrac{1}{2}$base $\times$ height

$= \dfrac{1}{2}BD \times$ height

$= \dfrac{1}{2}BD \times BF$ same height as $BFED$

$= \dfrac{1}{2}$area $BFED$

But $\triangle BCD$ is half of the rectangle $ABCD$, so that area $ABCD$ = area $BFED$.

(iv) Since the triangles ABD, ECD and FBC are similar, then

$$\frac{AB}{AD} = \frac{CE}{DE} \text{ and } \frac{AB}{AD} = \frac{BF}{CF}$$

the sides of similar triangles have the same ratios

Multiply these two:

$$\frac{AB}{AD}\frac{AB}{AD} = \frac{CE}{DE}\frac{BF}{CF}$$

But $BF = DE$

$BFED$ is a rectangle

So

$$\frac{(AB)^2}{(AD)^2} = \frac{CE}{CF}$$

cancelling BF with DE

The Angle Bisector Theorems

In the triangle ABC, the line AX bisects the angle at A. The theorem states that

$$\frac{AB}{AC} = \frac{BX}{XC}$$

The result is also true if the angle is bisected externally:

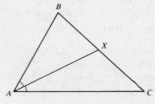

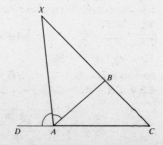

DAB is the exterior angle, which is bisected by AX.

Example

$PQ = 15$ cm, $QR = 12$ cm and $PR = 10$ cm. PS bisects angle QPR and PT bisects angle XPR. Calculate QS. RS and TS.

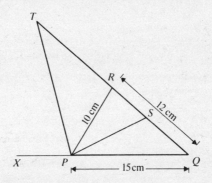

Answer

Use the angle bisector theorem in triangle PQR:

$$\frac{PQ}{PR} = \frac{QS}{RS}$$

so

$$\frac{15}{10} = \frac{QS}{RS}$$

Comments

putting in the given lengths

So S divides QR in the ratio $15:10$ which is the same as $3:2$.

$QR = 12$ cm which divides up as $7\cdot2$ and $4\cdot8$ divide 12 in the ratio 3:2

$QS = 7\cdot2$ cm, $RS = 4\cdot8$ cm,

$QS \cdot RS = 7\cdot2 \times 4\cdot8 = 34\cdot56$.

Use the exterior form of the theorem

$$\frac{PQ}{PR} = \frac{QT}{RT} \text{ so } QT \cdot RT = 3:2, \text{ so } QR = \tfrac{1}{3}QT$$

$12 = \tfrac{1}{3}QT, QT = 36$.

And so $RT = 36 - 12 = 24$

$TS = TR + RS = 24 + 3\cdot4 = 27\cdot4$ cm.

Section 12:
Circles and Their Properties

The proofs of the theorems in this section are not given here; they can be found in any standard textbook. This section concentrates on the use of the properties of circles.

Technical Terms

A line joining the centre of a circle to its circumference is called a *radius*. A line which joins two points on the circumference is called a *chord*. A chord that passes through the centre is a *diameter*. A line that cuts through the circle is a *secant*, and a line that touches the circle is a *tangent*. A chord divides the circle into a *major segment* and a *minor segment* which divide the circumference into a *major arc* and a *minor arc*.

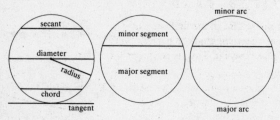

When doing a problem with circles, do not assume that chords are diameters, or that angles are right angles unless explicitly told. The centre of a circle is usually a clearly marked point on the diagram.

A chord meets the circle at two points. If these points are connected by radii to the centre of the circle, an angle is formed. This is called the *angle subtended* by the chord at the centre.

If the end points of the chord are joined to a third point on the circumference of the circle, the angle formed at this point is called the *angle subtended* by the chord at the *circumference*.

Circle properties

Property 1. The angle subtended by a chord at the circumference is the same no matter where the point is chosen on the circumference.

Property 2. The angle subtended by a chord at the centre is twice the angle subtended at the circumference. Since the angle subtended by a diameter at the centre is 180°, Property 2 leads to:

Property 3. The angle subtended by a diameter at the circumference is a right angle.

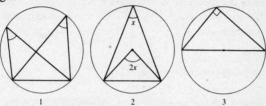

Property 4. The intersecting chord theorem: If AB and CD are two chords of a circle, that intersect at the point X, which may be inside or outside the circle, then

$$AX . XB = CX . XD$$

You can prove this, in the first case for example, by showing that the triangles ACX and BXD are similar. This uses Property 1.

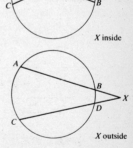

Property 5. The tangent secant theorem: If the chord CD above is allowed to drop so that it becomes a tangent to the circle, then CX and DX become equal. The property reduces to $AX . XB = CX^2$.

Properties 1 to 4 can be used backwards to show that given points lie on a circle. For example, if *A*, *B* and *C* are three points such that $A\hat{B}C = 90°$, then *B* lies on the circle with *A C* as diameter.

Taking the diameter *A C* as fixed, and allowing *B* to take all possible positions such that the angle is 90°, *B* sweeps out the circle. The path that *B* can follow is called its *locus*, and is a circle in this case. If, for example, the angle *A B C* is fixed at 60°, then the locus of *B* is an arc of the circle.

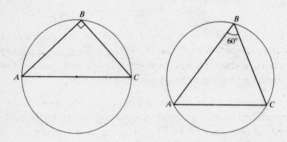

Another locus example: Take two fixed points *A* and *B*. The locus of all points which are the same distance from *A* and *B* is the perpendicular bisector of the line segment *A B*. That is the line perpendicular to *A B* and passing through its mid point. The reason is that for any point *C* on the bisector, $\triangle ABC$ is an isosceles triangle.

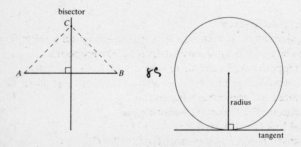

Property 6. A tangent is at right angles to the radius that it meets.

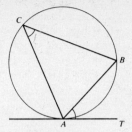

Property 7. The alternate segment theorem: In the diagram, AB is a chord of the circle, AT is a tangent at A and $\angle BCA$ is the angle subtended by this chord in the opposite segment. Then, the angle $\angle BCA$ is the same as the angle between the tangent and the chord.

Property 8. From a point outside the circle, two tangents can be drawn to the circle. The lengths of these tangents are the same. If the tangents are joined to the centre by radii, then the two triangles formed are congruent.

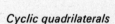

Cyclic quadrilaterals

If a quadrilateral is such that its four vertices lie on a circle, then it is said to be cyclic. A cyclic quadrilateral has the properties

  (i) Opposite angles add up to 180°;
     $\angle A + \angle C = 180°.$
  (ii) Since AC and BD are intersecting
     chords, then Property 4 above gives
     $AX.XC = BX.XD.$

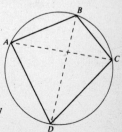

Note that Property 1 means that $D\hat{A}C = D\hat{B}C$ and so on.

    Either of these properties can be used to show that a quadrilateral is cyclic.

Examination questions and examples

1. *In the circle, Z X = 3 cm, Z Y = 4 cm and Z H = 6 cm. The length, in cm, of Z K is*
A $\frac{1}{2}$ B 1 C 2 D $4\frac{1}{2}$ E 8 (LON)

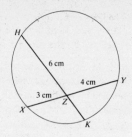

Answer

By the intersecting chord property, $HZ.ZK = XZ.ZY$

So $6ZK = 3 \times 4 = 12$
   $ZK = 2$

The answer is C.

2. *PQRS is a circle, centre O; POR is a diameter. x =*
A 20 B 40 C 50 D 60 E 70 (LON)

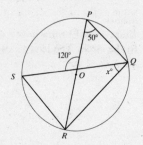

Answer

Angle $\angle PQS = 120° - 50° = 70°$, as the exterior angle = sum of opposite interior angles.
Since POR is a diameter, then $\angle PQR = 90°$ (Property 3)
And $x = 90° - \angle PQS = 90° - 70° = 20°$.
The answer is A.

3. *PM is the tangent at P to the circle, and PQ is a diameter. Then x must equal*
A u B v C w D y E z (LON)

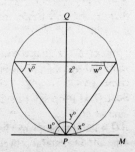

Answer

This is just the alternate segment theorem. The answer is $x = v$, which is answer **B**. The line PQ is irrelevant.

4. *In the figure, the points A, B and C are on the circumference of the circle centre O. The angle $AOC = 140°$ and AO is parallel to BC. Calculate the values of (a) d (b) e* (AEB)

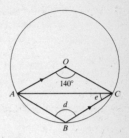

Answer

(a) Form the triangle APC where P is any point on the arc AC. Then the angle $APC = 70°$.

Comments

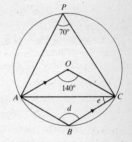

angle at centre =
2 × angle at circumference

$APCB$ is a cyclic quadrilateral, so that the opposite angles add to 180°.
$d = 180° - 70° = 110°$.

(b) AOC is an isosceles triangle, since AO and CO are radii of the circle.
So $\angle OAC = \angle OCA = \frac{1}{2}(180° - 140°)$
$= 20°$

AO is parallel to BC, so that
$e = \angle OAC = 20°$.

alternate angles

5. AB is the diameter of a
circle and BC is a tangent
at B such that $AB = BC$.
Prove that the mid point, M,
of AC lies on the circle and
that $\angle MBC = \angle MAB$.

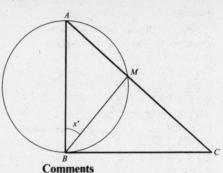

Answer

ABC is an isosceles triangle
BM is the median and so
$\angle AMB = 90°$
Since $\angle AMB$ is a right angle, M is
on the circle with diameter AB.
$\angle MBC = 90° - x°$
$\angle MAB = 90° - x°$
So $\angle MBC = \angle MAB$.

Comments

because $AB = BC$

only true for an *isosceles* triangle

see property 3, p. 137
tangent BC perpendicular to AB
since $\angle AMB = 90°$

6. *The two circles in the figure
cut at X and Y. The points R and S,
one on each circle, are such that
RXS is a straight line. The tangents
at R and S, to the circles on which they
lie, meet at P. The point T is on the circle
RXY such that RT is parallel to PS.*

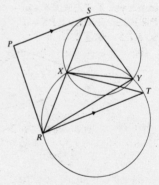

(a) Giving reasons which do not depend on measurement, explain why
(i) $P\hat{R}S + P\hat{S}R = R\hat{Y}S$
(ii) *PRYS is a cyclic quadrilateral*
(iii) $R\hat{P}S = R\hat{X}T$
*(b) If XY = 5 cm, and XY is produced to Z such that YZ = 4 cm,
calculate the length of the tangent from Z to either circle.* (AEB)

Answer

(a) (i) Using the alternate segment theorem in circle SYX with tangent PS and chord SX, $P\hat{S}R = S\hat{Y}X$.
Use the same theorem in the other circle, $P\hat{R}S = R\hat{Y}X$. Add the results:
$P\hat{R}S + P\hat{S}R = R\hat{Y}X + D\hat{Y}X = R\hat{Y}S$.

(ii) Since PSR is a triangle,
$P\hat{S}R + P\hat{R}S + R\hat{P}S = 180°$. But from (i) $P\hat{R}S + P\hat{S}R = R\hat{Y}S$, so that
$R\hat{Y}S + R\hat{P}S = 180$.
So $PRYS$ is cyclic.

(iii) PR is a tangent to the circle $XYTR$ and RX is a chord, so
$P\hat{R}X = R\hat{T}X = a°$, say.
$X\hat{Y}R = R\hat{T}X = a°$.
PS is a tangent to the circle XYS and XS is a chord, so $P\hat{S}R = S\hat{Y}X = b°$, say.
PS is parallel to RT, so $T\hat{R}S = P\hat{S}R = b°$.
In triangle XRT, $R\hat{X}T + a° + b° = 180°$.
$PRYS$ is cyclic, so $R\hat{P}S + a° + b° = 180°$.
So $R\hat{P}S = R\hat{X}T$.

(b)

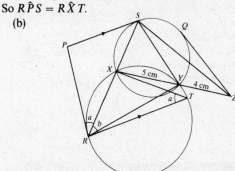

From the tangent secant property
$XZ.YZ = ZQ^2$, so $36 = ZQ^2$
$$ZQ = 6$$
The length of tangent ZQ is 6 cm.

Comments

the opposite angles of a cyclic quad add up to 180°

both are subtended by the chord XR

alternate angles

draw a new diagram (see p. 137)

Section 13: Ruler and Compass Constructions

General points: Use a sharp HB pencil, and draw the construction lines cleanly. Show *all* your construction lines, as your methods are being tested by the examiner.

The final drawing should be clear to follow, and not disfigured by repeated rubbing out.

Make sure that your compasses are tightly screwed together.

Make a scale line at the top or bottom of the page, and use it for setting the compasses to the required lengths when constructing.

Constructions

1. Bisector of a given angle.
Set the compasses to a suitable separation.
Draw an arc with centre at the vertex, to cut both the lines.
With the same radius, and using these marks as centres, draw arcs which intersect between the lines. Joining this point of intersection to the vertex gives the bisector.

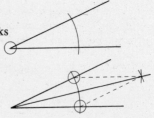

2. Perpendicular bisector of a line segment.
Set the compasses to a separation greater than half the length of the segment.
Using the end points as centres, draw arcs above and below the line segment.
Join the two crosses formed where the arcs intersect. This line is the perpendicular bisector.

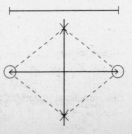

3. Erecting a perpendicular from a given point on a line.

With the given point as centre, mark off
two points on the line either side.
Bisect this new line segment as in 2. The
bisector is the required perpendicular.

4. Dropping a perpendicular from a point to a line.

With the given point as centre, draw arcs
to cut the line in two places.
Construct the perpendicular of this segment;
this is the required perpendicular.

5. Drawing a line through a given point and parallel to a given line.

Mark off two points on the line.
Set the compasses to the distance between
these points.
Draw an arc with centre at the given
point.
Set the compasses to the distance from the
given point to one of the points on the
line.
Draw an arc from the other point on the
line to cut the first arc. Joining the given
point to this point of intersection gives the
parallel line.

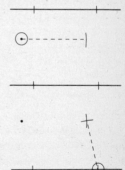

6. Copying a given angle.
With your centre the vertex of the angle
to be copied, draw an arc to cut the sides.
Draw a line, and mark a point on it.
With the same compass setting, draw an
arc centred on the marked point.
Set the compasses to the distance between
the points where the arc cuts the sides of
the original angle. With the same setting
and your centre the point where the arc
cuts the base of the new angle, draw an
arc to cut the first arc. Joining the point
of intersection to the mark on the base
line gives the angle.

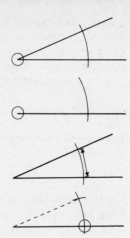

7. Special angles.
An angle of 90° can be made by constructing perpendiculars, as in 3.
Bisecting this angle gives 45°.
An angle of 135° can be made by constructing a 45° on to a 90°.
An angle of 60° can be made by constructing an equilateral triangle:
Draw a base line.
Setting the compasses to the length
of this base, draw arcs from the end points
to intersect. The point of intersection is
the third vertex of the triangle.
Bisecting the 60° gives 30°,
bisecting 30° gives 15°.

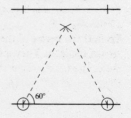

8. Constructing a triangle.
  (a) With given sides:
Mark off one of the lengths on the base
line.
With the compasses set to one of the other
lengths draw an arc from an end point of
the base.

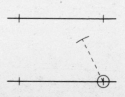

With the other end of the base as centre,
draw an arc with radius equal to the third
length. The point of intersection of the
two arcs is the third vertex.

(b) With two sides and the included
angle:
Draw the base line the same as one of the
given lengths.

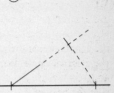

Copy the given angle onto this side, and mark off the second given length
along it.

(c) With two given angles and the
included side:
Draw the base to the given length.
Copy the angles at the ends of the base. Where the sides of the two
angles intersect is the third vertex.

*9. A circle passing through three given points (the circumscribed circle of
a triangle).*
To find the centre of the circle, construct the perpendicular bisectors of
two of the sides. They meet at the centre. The radius is the distance from
the centre to any of the three points of the triangle.

*10. A circle touching all three sides of a given triangle
(the inscribed circle).*
To find the centre, construct the bisectors of two of the angles. From
this centre, drop a perpendicular to one of the sides of the triangle. The
length of this perpendicular is the radius of the circle.

*11. Dividing a line segment into a given
number of equal pieces.*
Draw a line at an angle to the given line.
Choosing any compass setting, mark off
equal divisions on this line, to the required
number.
Join the last division on the oblique line to
the end of the given line segment.
Construct a line parallel to this line and
passing through the next division on the
oblique line. Repeat until all the divisions
are joined to the base line. The parallel
lines divide the base line into the required
pieces.

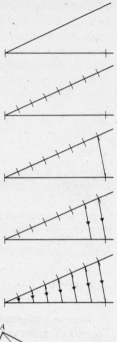

*12. A triangle equal in area to a given
quadrilateral ABCD.*
Draw a diagonal of the quadrilateral.
Construct the line through *B* parallel to
the diagonal *AC*. This line meets *DC* at *P*.
The triangle *APD* is the required one.

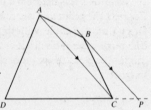

*13. A square equal in area to a given
rectangle ABCD.*
Extend *AB* to *E* so that *BE = BC*.
Cut the segment *AE* in half at *O*, and
draw a semicircle centred on *O* with *OA*
as radius. The semicircle meets *BC* at *X*,
BX is one side of the required square.

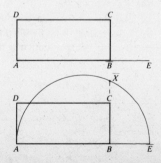

14. To draw the arc of a circle containing a given angle.
Draw the base line *A B* with the given
angle as in the figure.
Construct the perpendicular *A T* and the
bisector *A B*, which intersect at the centre
of the circle. The radius is *O A*.

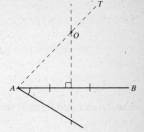

15. To draw a tangent at a given point on a circle.
Join the given point to the centre with a
radius.
Construct a perpendicular to this radius at
the given point. This is the tangent.

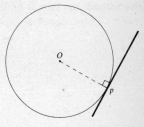

16. To draw a tangent from a point outside a circle to the circle.
Connect the point and the centre of the circle.
Draw a second circle, with this line as diameter.
The point where this circle cuts the
original circle is the point of contact of the
tangent.

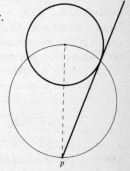

Section 14:
Sines, Cosines and Tangents

The Trigonometric Ratios

In the right-angled triangle ABC, the ratios
$\frac{AB}{AC}$, $\frac{BC}{AC}$ and $\frac{BC}{AB}$ do not depend on the size
of the triangle, but only on the size of the
angles. These are called the *trigonometric
ratios*:

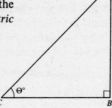

$$\sin \theta = \frac{AB}{AC} \quad \cos \theta = \frac{BC}{AC} \quad \tan \theta = \frac{AB}{BC}.$$

Sin is short for sine, cos for cosine and tan for tangent.

It is easier to remember these ratios if the sides of the triangle are
labelled as $AB = $ side *opposite* the angle θ

$AC = $ *hypotenuse* (side opposite the 90°)

and $BC = $ *adjacent* side (joins the angle θ to the 90°)

Then the ratios can be written as

$$\sin \theta = \frac{\text{opposite}}{\text{hypotenuse}} \quad \cos \theta = \frac{\text{adjacent}}{\text{hypotenuse}} \quad \tan \theta = \frac{\text{opposite}}{\text{adjacent}}$$

which, in turn, can be remembered by their initials as

SOH   CAH   TOA

For given angles, the values of these ratios can be found from tables or
a calculator.

The ratios are used to find the sides of triangles.

Examples *1. Given that cos 70° = 0·34, sin 70° = 0·94 and tan 70° = 2·75, the length, in cm, of YZ is*
A 2·94   B 3·4   C 7·0   D 9·4   E 27·5 (LON)

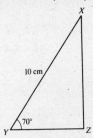

Answer YZ is the adjacent side, and the hypotenuse is known, so the cosine is the useful ratio here (**CAH**).
$\cos 70° = \frac{YZ}{10}$ from the triangle. But $\cos 70° = 0·34$
So $0·34 = \frac{YZ}{10}$ giving $YZ = 3·4$ cm. Answer **B**.

2. In the figure, the trapezium PQRS has PS parallel to QR, QR = 10 cm, RS = 6 cm, QS = 8 cm and angle QSR = angle QPS = 90°. Write down
(a) sin x°
(b) cos x°
and hence calculate
(c) the length of PQ
(d) the length of PS
(e) the area of the trapezium PQRS. (AEB)

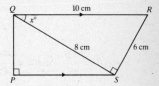

Answer

(a) $\sin x° = \dfrac{\text{opposite}}{\text{hypotenuse}} = \dfrac{6}{10} = 0·6$

(b) $\cos x° = \dfrac{\text{adjacent}}{\text{hypotenuse}} = \dfrac{8}{10} = 0·8$

(c) Since QR is parallel to PS, $\angle RQS = \angle QSP$, so $\angle QSP = x°$. In triangle PQS, $\sin x° = \frac{PQ}{8}$
So $PQ = 8\sin x° = 8 \times 0·6 = 4·8$ cm.

(d) In the same triangle $\cos x° = \frac{PS}{8}$
So $PS = 8\cos x° = 8 \times 0·8 = 6·4$ cm.

(e) The area of the triangle PQS is $\frac{1}{2} \times PS \times QP$

$$= \frac{1}{2} \times 6{\cdot}4 \times 4{\cdot}8$$

$$= 15{\cdot}36$$

The area of the triangle QSR is $\frac{1}{2} \times QS \times SR$

$$= \frac{1}{2} \times 8 \times 6 = 24$$

So the combined area is $39{\cdot}36$ cm^2.

The trigonometric ratios can also be used to find the angles of a triangle. If the sine ratio is known, for example, then the angle can be found using either sine tables or a calculator.

Example Find the angle at A in the triangle ABC.

Answer The side opposite the angle is 3 cm, and the hypotenuse is 4 cm, so

$$\sin A = \frac{\text{opposite}}{\text{hypotenuse}} = \frac{3}{4} = 0{\cdot}75$$

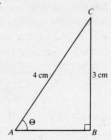

If you are using tables, look up to see which angle corresponds to $0{\cdot}75$. If you are using a calculator, key in $0{\cdot}75$ and then press the INV (or ARC) key followed by the SIN key. The answer is $48{\cdot}59°$.

Degrees and minutes

The answer to the last example was written as a decimal of a degree; another way to express it is in degrees and minutes. There are 60 minutes in a degree, so that a minute is a sixtieth of a degree. To convert the decimal part of an angle to minutes, multiply by 60. So $0{\cdot}59° = 0{\cdot}59 \times 60$ minutes, which is 35 minutes. So $48{\cdot}59° = 48° \, 35'$ (to the nearest minute), where the ′ denotes minutes.

If an angle is given in degrees and minutes, and you want to write it in decimals of degrees, then divide the minutes by 60. So, $23° \, 56' = 23{\cdot}93°$ since $56 \div 60 = 0{\cdot}93$ to 2 significant figures.

It may be useful to remember the following table for sin, cos and tan of common angles:

	sin	cos	tan
0°	0	1	0
30°	$\dfrac{1}{2}$	$\dfrac{\sqrt{3}}{2}$	$\dfrac{1}{\sqrt{3}}$
45°	$\dfrac{1}{\sqrt{2}}$	$\dfrac{1}{\sqrt{2}}$	1
60°	$\dfrac{\sqrt{3}}{2}$	$\dfrac{1}{2}$	$\sqrt{3}$
90°	1	0	∞

Angles greater than 90°

It is not possible to fit an obtuse angle into a right-angled triangle because the angles must all add up to 180°. Hence it is not possible to define sine, cosine and tangent for these angles by putting them in right-angled triangles. A more general method is needed.

The angle is measured from the x-axis in an anti-clockwise direction, (step 1). Take the *acute* angle that the line makes with the x-axis.

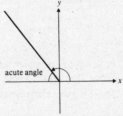

Find the sin, cos and tan of this angle from tables (or calculator) (step 2). Put a + or − in front of the answer to step 1 according to the following scheme:

second quadrant sine +	First quadrant all +
tangent + third quadrant	cosine + fourth quadrant

where all the ratios have a + in the first quadrant (0°–90°); only the sin has a + in the second quadrant (90°–180°); only the tan has a + in the third quadrant (180°–270°); and only the cos has a + in the fourth quadrant (270°–360°).

Example 1. Find the sin, cos and tan of
the angle 120°

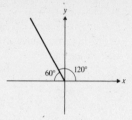

Answer The line makes the acute angle 60°
with the *x*-axis, and sin 60° = 0·8660
$$\cos 60° = 0·5000$$
$$\tan 60° = 1·7320$$

The angle is in the second quadrant (as it is between 90° and 180°) so
that the sin is positive.

so sin 120° = 0·8660

$$\cos 120° = -0·5000$$
$$\tan 120° = -1·7320$$

2. Find the sin, cos and tan of the angle 279°.

Answer The acute is 81°. The angle is in the fourth quadrant.

sin 81° = 0·9877   so sin 279° = −0·9877

cos 81° = 0·1564   so cos 279° = 0·1564

tan 81° = 6·3138   so tan 279° = −6·3138

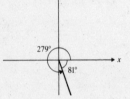

Notice that, while sin and cos can only take values between −1 and 1,
tan can take any value. In other words, the range of sin and cos is
−1 ⩽ *y* ⩽ +1, while the range of tan is all the real numbers. You may
be asked to find angles from given sin, cos or tan values. See p. 164.

The Sine and Cosine Rules

When you have a right-angled triangle, you can use Pythagoras and
the definitions of sines and cosines to work out distances. If the triangle is
not right angled then these cannot be used. Fortunately there are some
other formulae to use. These are:

(i) The sine rule

For any triangle ABC, using the standard notation for the sides and angles, the sine rule states that

$$\frac{\sin A}{a} = \frac{\sin B}{b} = \frac{\sin C}{c}$$

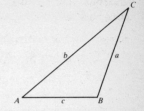

This is most useful when one of the sides is known, and a couple of angles. The known side must be opposite a known angle to be useful.

Example ABC is a triangle with $AB = 10$ cm, $\angle ABC = 50°$, $\angle ACB = 27°$. Calculate BC.

Answer In the diagram you can see that all the angles are known, as the third angle is $180° - 50° - 27° = 103°$.
From the sin rule

$$\frac{\sin 103°}{a} = \frac{\sin 50°}{b} = \frac{\sin 27°}{c}$$

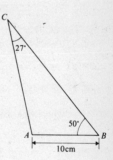

$BC = a$, $AB = c = 10$. Using the first and last pair

$$\frac{\sin 103°}{a} = \frac{\sin 27°}{10} \text{ so } a = \frac{10 \sin 103°}{\sin 27°}$$

$$a = \frac{10 \times 0{\cdot}9744}{0{\cdot}4540} = 21{\cdot}46.$$

$BC = 21{\cdot}5$ cm (to one decimal place).

(ii) The cosine rule

This can be used to find a third side of a triangle when the other two sides and an angle are known, or to find an angle when all three sides are known. The rule is:

$$a^2 = b^2 + c^2 - 2bc\cos A$$

Two other versions can be obtained by
changing the letters around, so

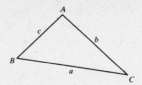

$$b^2 = a^2 + c^2 - 2ac\cos B$$

and $\quad c^2 = a^2 + b^2 - 2ab\cos C$

The version you should use depends on which side is to be found; if b is
needed, for example, the second version is the right one.

Example *ABCD is a quadrilateral in which $AB = 7$ cm, $BC = 6$ cm,
$DA = 4$ cm, the angle $BAD = 60°$ and the angle $BCD = 90°$. Calculate:*

(i) *The lengths of BD and CD*

(ii) *The size of the angle ADC.* (AEB)

Answer

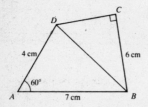

(i) In triangle ABD, using the cosine
rule,

$$DB^2 = 4^2 + 7^2 - (2 \times 4 \times 7 \times \cos 60°)$$
$$= 16 + 49 - (56 \times 0\cdot5)$$
$$= 65 - 28$$
$$= 37$$

$$BD = \sqrt{37} = 6\cdot08 \text{ cm.}$$

BCD is a right-angled triangle, and
two of the sides are known. Pythagoras'
Theorem gives

$$BD^2 = CD^2 + 6^2$$
$$CD^2 = BD^2 - 6^2$$
$$= 37 - 36$$
$$= 1$$
so $CD = 1$ cm.

Comments

first draw the diagram from
the information given

$\cos 60° = 0\cdot5$

using calculator or tables
for square root

rearranging
as $BD^2 = 37$
(from above)

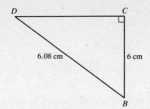

(ii) To find $A\hat{D}C$, find $A\hat{D}B$ and $B\hat{D}C$
separately. In the right-angled triangle
BCD, $\tan D = \frac{6}{1} = 6$, so $BDC = 80\cdot53°$ calculator
Using the sin rule in triangle ADB

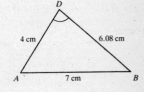

$$\frac{\sin 60°}{6\cdot08} = \frac{\sin D}{7}$$

$$\sin D = \frac{7\sin 60°}{6\cdot08} = 0\cdot9971$$

so $\angle ADB = 85\cdot61°$
The combined angle $\angle ADC$ is $166\cdot14°$.   adding the two angles

Formula for the area of a triangle
When two sides and the included angle of a triangle are known, the area
can be worked out from the formula

$$\text{area} = \tfrac{1}{2}ab\sin C$$

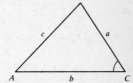

where C is the known angle.
(Similarly, $\tfrac{1}{2}bc\sin A$ or $\tfrac{1}{2}ac\sin B$.)

Applications

1. Angles of elevation and depression
If you want to find the height of a tree, it is not always practical to climb
the tree with a tape measure! The trigonometric ratios give an easier
method. Assuming that the tree stands vertically, then the top and base of
the tree form a right-angled triangle with any other point on the ground.
Mark a point on the ground, and measure the distance from the mark to
the base of the tree. Measure the angle that the top of the tree makes at

this point, which is called the *angle of elevation* of the top of the tree from that point.

The opposite and adjacent sides of the triangle are involved. The opposite side is the height which is to be found. The adjacent side is the distance along the ground. The tan of the angle can now be found (T O A).

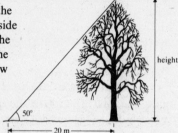

For example, if the distance measured along the ground is 20 m, and the angle of elevation is found to be 50°, then

$$\tan 50° = \frac{\text{height}}{20}$$

$$\text{height} = 20\tan 50°$$

$$= 20 \times 1 \cdot 1918$$

$$= 23 \cdot 84$$

The height of the tree must be 23·84 m.

When doing this type of calculation, write down all the steps; it makes it easier to check for mistakes.

If you have to look down at something, the angle that your line of sight makes with the horizontal is the *angle of depression*.

Example *A man stands on horizontal ground with his feet 50 m from the base of a vertical tower. He observes the angle of elevation of the top of the tower to be 12° and the angle of depression of the base of the tower to be 2°. Find, in metres correct to one decimal place, the height of the tower.* (LON)

Answer

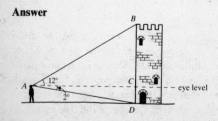

Comments
the angles are measured from eye level

In triangle ABC, $\tan 12° = \frac{BC}{50}$ angle of elevation of top
so $BC = 50 \tan 12° = 50 \times 0·2126$
$\qquad\qquad\quad = 10·63$
In triangle ACD, $\tan 2° = \frac{CD}{50}$ angle of depression of base
so $CD = 50 \tan 2° = 50 \times 0·0349$
$\qquad\qquad\quad = 1·75$
The total height is 12·38.   adding the two results
To one decimal place, the height is 12·4 m.   required accuracy

In this type of question, it is very important to draw a good diagram to guide your working. Once the diagram has been drawn you can usually see how to carry on.

If you are using a calculator, make sure that it is set to *degrees*. Most calculators have radians as an alternative unit of angle, but you will not need to use them. If you are using tables, make sure that you are looking up figures in the right ones.

2. Bearings

These are used to describe positions. Looking from a fixed reference point to the object point, the angle that the line of sight makes with the North direction is called the bearing. This angle is measured in a *clockwise* direction from North.
It is measured in degrees, and is always written with 3 figures before the decimal point, so that the angle of 26° would be written as 026°.
In the diagram, the bearing of B from A is 030°.

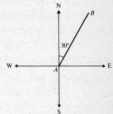

To find the corresponding bearing of A from B, add this angle to 180°, to get 210°.

It is important to specify the reference point when giving a bearing. (Note that the exact position of the object B is determined when the distance AB is also known.)

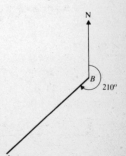

Example The bearing of *S* from *P* is
045°; the bearing of *S* from *Q* is 330°.
S is the point of intersection of the
two reference lines.

Bearings are used for navigating at sea.

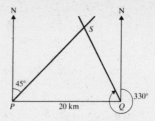

Example *A ship is sailing at a steady speed on a course of 045°. From an
observation post P it is sighted passing through a point A, 8 km due north
of P, and 50 minutes later it passes through a point B on a bearing of
033° 28′ from P. Calculate:*

   (i) The distance A B

  (ii) The speed of the ship.

   *At B the ship alters course to due east and then sails to a point D, 5 km
east of B. Calculate:*

 (iii) How far D is east of A

 (iv) The bearing of D from P, correct to the nearest degree. (A E B)

Answer

Comments
it is essential to draw a
diagram first

(i) Angle $PAB = 180° - 45° = 135°$

so $ABP = 180° - 135° - 33°28′$

       $= 11°32′$

Using the sin rule   see p. 155

$$\frac{\sin 33°28′}{AB} = \frac{\sin 11°32′}{8}$$

$$AB = \frac{8\sin 33°\,28'}{\sin 11°\,32'} \qquad \text{cross multiplying}$$

$$= \frac{8\sin 33\cdot47°}{\sin 11\cdot53°} \qquad \text{convert to decimals}$$

$$= \frac{8 \times 0\cdot5515}{0\cdot1999} \qquad \text{look up in sin tables}$$

$$AB = 22\cdot1 \text{ km}$$

(ii) speed = distance ÷ time   see p. 100

distance = $AB = 22\cdot1$ km

$$\text{time} = 50 \text{ mins} = \frac{50}{60} \text{ hours} \qquad \text{match units}$$

$$= 0\cdot83 \text{ hours}$$

speed = $22\cdot1 \div 0\cdot83 = 26\cdot6$ km/h.

(iii)   draw a new diagram

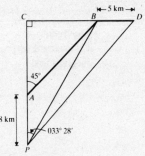

Distance of D east of A is CD.

$$CD = CB + BD = CB + 5 \qquad ABC \text{ is a right-angled}$$
triangle

$$\frac{CB}{AB} = \sin 45°$$

So $CB = AB\sin 45° = 22\cdot1 \times 0\cdot7071$
$$= 15\cdot6 \text{ km}$$

$$CD = 15\cdot6 + 5 = 20\cdot6$$

D is $20\cdot6$ km east of A.

(iv) The bearing is angle $C\,P\,D$.

$$\frac{A\,C}{A\,B} = \cos 45° \text{ so that}$$

$$A\,C = A\,B\cos 45° = 15·6$$

So $P\,C = 15·6 + 8 = 23·6$

$$\tan (C\,\hat{P}\,D) = \frac{D\,C}{C\,P} = \frac{20·6}{23·6}$$
$$= 0·8729$$

So $C\,\hat{P}\,D = 41·1°$ calculator INV TAN or
tables

The bearing of D from P is 041° to
the nearest degree.

Latitude and Longitude

These terms are used to describe the positions of points on the surface of
the earth, which is taken to be a sphere of radius 6 400 km.

The *axis* of the earth is a line joining the North and South poles. The
plane through the centre which is perpendicular to the axis cuts the surface
to form a circle. This circle is the *equator*.

Circles on the surface which are parallel to the equator are called circles
of *latitude*, and are specified by an angle.

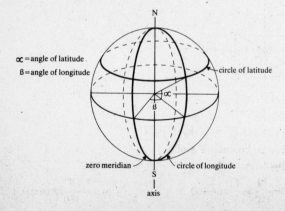

The angle that the line joining a point on a circle of latitude to the centre makes with the plane of the equator is called the angle of latitude. The equator has zero angle of latitude; points to the North have angles of latitude given as so many degrees North, while those to the South have the word South after the angle.

Circles with their centre the same as the centre of the earth and which pass through the poles are called Great Circles, meridians or *circles of longitude*. One of these circles is taken as the zero meridian, which has zero angle of longitude. For another circle of longitude, the angle between this circle and the zero meridian is the angle of longitude, which is specified as East or West. The angles of latitude and longitude of a point on the surface of the earth are the angles of the corresponding circles of latitude and longitude that the point lies on.

The point is found by taking the point of intersection of its circles of latitude and longitude.

Example *Two places, X and Y, on the surface of the earth, both lie on the equator. X is on longitude 30° W and Y is on longitude 40° E. Calculate the shorter distance between X and Y measured along the equator.*

A third place Z has the same longitude as Y and the arc X Y equals the arc Y Z. Calculate the radius of the circle of latitude through Z. (Take the earth to be a sphere of radius 6 400 km, and π to be $\frac{22}{7}$.) (A E B)

Answer

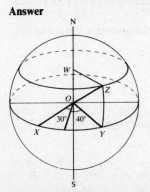

Comments
diagram first

The total angle between X and Y
on the equator is 70°.

Arc $X Y = \dfrac{70}{180} \times \dfrac{22}{7} \times 6\,400$
$\qquad\qquad\qquad$ arc $= \dfrac{\theta}{180}\pi r$ (see p. 113)

$$= \frac{22 \times 6400}{18} \text{ km}$$

$$= 7822 \cdot 2 \text{ km}$$

Let the sector $O\,YZ$ contain an angle of θ.

Arc $YZ = \text{arc } XY = 7822 \cdot 2 \text{ km}$

So $\theta = \dfrac{180 \times 7822 \cdot 2 \times 7}{22 \times 6400}$ rearranging arc formula

$\quad\quad = 70$

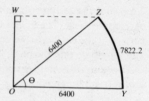

Z has angle of latitude $70°$.

In triangle OZW,

$$\sin (90° - 70°) = \frac{WZ}{6400}$$

so $WZ = 6400\sin 20°$

$\quad\quad\quad = 2189 \text{ km}.$

Three-dimensional Problems

Sines and cosines are used to find distances and angles in three-dimensional problems. It is essential to draw enough diagrams to see how to calculate the required quantities. Draw three-dimensional and plan views.

Example *A horizontal building plot is in the shape of a quadrilateral* $ABCD$ *where* $AB = 73 \cdot 2$ m, $BD = 48 \cdot 3$ m, *the angle* $ABD = 118°42'$, *the angle* $BDC = 78°42'$ *and the angle* $BCD = 67°12'$. *A vertical radio mast* BT *stands at the corner B of the plot as shown in the figure. Calculate:*

(i) The height of the radio mast BT, *if the angle of elevation of T from A is* $16°24'$

(ii) The angle of elevation of T from D
(iii) The length of A D
(iv) The length of B C. (AEB)

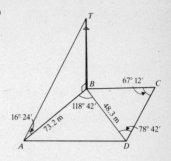

Answer

(i) Triangle ABT

Comments

draw a plan

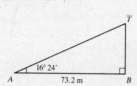

$$\tan 16° 24' = \frac{BT}{73\cdot 2}$$

so $\qquad BT = 73\cdot 2 \times \tan 16° 24'$

$\qquad\qquad = 73\cdot 2 \times 0\cdot 2943$

$\qquad\qquad = 21\cdot 5$

The mast is 21·5 m high.

(ii) Triangle TBD

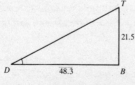

$$\tan D = \frac{BT}{BD} = \frac{21\cdot 5}{48\cdot 3} = 0\cdot 4451$$

so $\qquad D = 24\cdot 0°$ $\qquad\qquad\qquad$ calculator

The angle of elevation is 24°.

(iii) Use the cos rule in the
triangle ABD

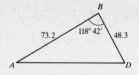

$$AD^2 = 73{\cdot}2^2 + 48{\cdot}3^2 - 2(73{\cdot}2)(48{\cdot}3)\cos 118° 42' \qquad \text{see p. 155}$$

$$= 5\,358{\cdot}2 + 2\,332{\cdot}9 - 2(73{\cdot}2)(48{\cdot}3)(-0{\cdot}4802) \qquad \text{see p. 153}$$

$$= 11\,086{\cdot}7$$

so $AD = 105{\cdot}3.$ square root

(iv) Use the sin rule in triangle BCD

$$\frac{\sin 67° 12'}{48{\cdot}3} = \frac{\sin 78° 42'}{BC}$$

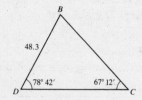

$$BC = \frac{0{\cdot}9806 \times 48{\cdot}3}{0{\cdot}9219} \qquad \text{putting in sines}$$

$$= 51{\cdot}4 \text{ m.}$$

Section 15: Statistics

What to do with Numerical Data

The result of a statistical survey is a collection of numbers, which are usually then put into a table. For example, they could be the heights or ages of a group of people.

Example The numbers of candidates obtaining each grade in a mathematics examination one year were

grade	A	B	C	D	E	U
number of candidates	2 780	4 360	6 370	1 600	1 380	3 560

However, it is not easy for the average person to deduce much from a large set of numbers. Information about the data can be more easily drawn from a diagram. One form of statistical diagram is:

The bar chart
For each grade a strip (bar) with height representing the number of candidates is drawn. The number for each grade is called its *frequency*. Frequency is usually plotted vertically on the diagram, but could equally well be measured horizontally. The bars are spaced out to make the table easier to read.

The table enables you to see the relative frequencies of the grades: for example, you can see that almost twice as many people got grade C as got grade U.

If you want to see what proportion of the candidates got each grade, the bars can be placed one after the other in a long strip. This produces a cumulative diagram.

Frequency bar chart

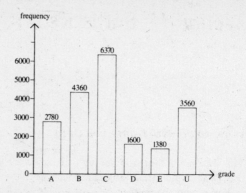

Cumulative frequency strip

A	B	C	D	E	U
2 780	4 360	6 370	1 600	1 380	3 560

Another type of chart is:

The pie chart

A circle is divided up with angles representing the frequencies.

To draw the chart, the % frequencies for each grade must be calculated, and then these percentages of 360° give the angles of the sectors.

grade	frequency	%	angle
A	2 780	13·9	50
B	4 360	21·8	78
C	6 370	31·8	114
D	1 600	8·0	29
E	1 380	6·9	25
U	3 560	17·8	64
totals	20 050	100·2	360

The totals give a check on the calculations. The percentages should add up to 100, and the angles to 360°. Because the figures are rounded up the totals may be slightly out, as for the percentages here.

Now draw a circle of suitable radius. Mark a radius as reference, and measure the angles round the circle (using a protractor).

For each sector, write in the grade and % or angle.

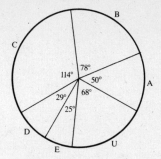

Pie chart

This was an example of *discrete* data. The quantity being measured, the grades, could only take a certain number of different values which are not themselves numbers (A, B, C, D, E, U).

When the quantity to be measured can take any value within a given range, such as height or weight, the data are said to be *continuous*. For continuous data, a type of bar chart called a *histogram* can be drawn. This is like a bar chart except that

    (i) the horizontal axis represents numerical data;

    (ii) there are no spaces between the strips;

    (iii) frequency is represented by the area of each strip, not the height.

If all the strips have the same width, then (iii) has no effect. However, if some of the strips are wider than the others, then their heights must be scaled down accordingly.

Example A manufacturer of electric light bulbs tests a sample of 80 bulbs. He finds that the lives of these bulbs are distributed as shown in the table:

length of life in hours		number of bulbs
at least	less than	
1 100	1 200	5
1 200	1 300	10
1 300	1 400	13
1 400	1 500	18
1 500	1 600	15
1 600	1 700	7
1 700	2 000	12

Notice that the lengths of life are given as *ranges* of values.

Histogram

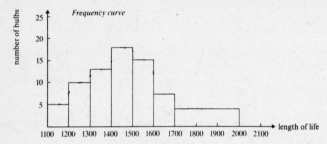

The last strip is three times as wide as the others, so the frequency must be divided by three to give the height of the strip. $12 \div 3 = 4$. The *area* of the strip is 12.

The scaling is done because it seems more natural to associate importance with the size, or area, of the strip. If the last strip were given a height of 12, then it would seem that more bulbs were lasting for 2 000 hours than actually did.

The life times were given as ranges, 1 100 to 1 200 for example. Often the mid point of the range is taken to represent the whole range. For the range 1 100–1 200, the *mid range* (mid interval value) is 1150.

If the points on top of the strips above the mid ranges are joined, you get a *frequency curve*.

Frequency curve

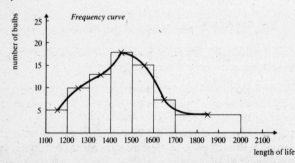

If the frequencies are added successively, the *cumulative frequencies* are obtained. A cumulative frequency curve can then be drawn, by plotting the cumulative frequency above the *upper end point* of each range.

Table to find cumulative frequencies (cumf)

range	frequency	cumf
1 100–1 200	5	5
1 200–1 300	10	5 + 10 = 15
1 300–1 400	13	15 + 13 = 28
1 400–1 500	18	28 + 18 = 46
1 500–1 600	15	46 + 18 = 61
1 600–1 700	7	61 + 7 = 68
1 700–2 000	12	68 + 12 = 80

The final cumf figure should be the total frequency.

Cumulative frequency curve

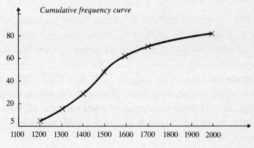

Statistical Averages

A table of data can also be used to find *average* values which may be used to represent the whole data. There are three types:

1. *The mean* is the usual arithmetical average. Total the numbers and then divide by the number of numbers. For example, the average of the 10 numbers 1, 2, 1, 3, 4, 2, 1, 5, 4, 1 is $\frac{1+2+1+3+4+2+1+5+4+1}{10} = 2.4$.

When the data are given in the form of a frequency table, then the numbers must be multiplied by their frequencies before adding, and then the total divided by the total frequency.

2. *The median* is the middle number when a list is arranged in order (increasing or decreasing).

When the numbers above are put into increasing order we get:

$$1, 1, 1, 1, 2, 2, 3, 4, 4, 5.$$

But, since there are ten numbers, there is no middle one! When this happens, take the average of the two middle ones. These are both 2, so that the average is also 2. The median is 2.

3. *The mode* is the number occurring the most number of times; it has the highest frequency. For the data above, it is the number 1 which occurs 4 times.

Example *The table shows an analysis of the number of goals scored in 80 football matches.*

Goals per match	0	1	2	3	4	5	6
Frequency of matches	8	10	21	18	10	8	5

(a) Write down the modal number of goals per match.
(b) Find the median number of goals per match.
(c) Calculate the mean number of goals per match.
When the results of another 20 matches were taken into account, the mean number of goals scored per match for all the matches became 2·5.
(d) Calculate the mean number of goals per match for the 20 matches.

(AEB)

Answer

(a) The modal number, or mode, is the one with the highest frequency. This is 2, which has a frequency of 21.

(b) The median is best found from the cumulative frequency table:

goals	0	1	2	3	4	5	6
frequency	8	10	21	18	10	8	5
cumf	8	18	39	57	67	75	80

The total is even, so that the median is the average of the two middle ones, the 40th and 41st ones. The cumf first goes over these values for 3 goals. The median is 3. (For any cumulative frequency table, the median corresponds to the first cumf which is larger than half of the total frequency.)

(c) To calculate the mean, multiply the numbers by the frequencies and add. Then divide by the total frequency, which is 80.

$$\text{mean} = \frac{0 \times 8 + 1 \times 10 + 2 \times 21 + 3 \times 18 + 4 \times 10 + 5 \times 8 + 6 \times 5}{80}$$

$$= \frac{216}{80} = 2\text{·}75.$$

(d) This depends on using the formula mean $= \frac{\text{total}}{\text{total freq.}}$ repeatedly.
The mean of the 20 matches = total for $20 \div 20$.
The total of the first 80 matches is 216. The mean of all 100 matches is 2·5, so that the total for these matches was $2\text{·}5 \times 100 = 250$. The total for the other 20 matches must have been $250 - 216 = 34$. The average for the 20 matches was $\frac{34}{20} = 1\text{·}7$ goals.

The median can also be found from the cumulative frequency curve. The median is half-way, which corresponds to a cumf which is 50% of the total. Draw a line at 50% of the total frequency to cut the curve. The corresponding figure on the *x*-axis is the median. The median is called the *50th percentile*. Other percentiles are the 25th percentile, *or lower quartile*, corresponding to 25% of the total, and the 75th percentile, or *upper quartile*, corresponding to 75% of the total.

The difference between the two quartiles is called the *inter quartile range*.

Example *The frequency table below relates to the speeds of 160 vehicles passing a particular point on the main road.*

speed v (mph)	$v \leqslant 15$	$15 < v \leqslant 20$	$20 < v \leqslant 25$	$25 < v \leqslant 30$	$30 < v \leqslant 35$
frequency	0	2	3	22	30

speed	$35 < v \leqslant 40$	$40 < v \leqslant 45$	$45 < v \leqslant 50$	$50 < v \leqslant 55$	$55 < v \leqslant 60$
frequency	40	26	22	10	5

Calculate an estimate of the mean. Prepare a cumulative frequency table and draw the corresponding cumulative frequency diagram. From your diagram write down the median and upper and lower quartiles. (OXF)

Answer

speed	mid range	frequency	cumf	mid range × frequency
0–15	7·5	0	0	0
15–20	17·5	2	2	35
20–25	22·5	3	5	67·5
25–30	27·5	22	27	605
30–35	32·5	30	57	975
35–40	37·5	40	97	1 500
40–45	42·5	26	123	1 105
45–50	47·5	22	145	1 045
50–55	52·5	10	155	525
55–60	57·5	5	160	287·5
totals		160		6 145

Remember that to find the mean, the numbers must be multiplied by the frequencies. The mid ranges are taken to represent the ranges.

The mean is $\frac{6145}{160} = 38\cdot4$

Cumulative frequency diagram:

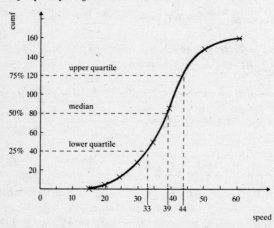

The median corresponds to 50% on the frequency axis. 50% of 160 is 80 which corresponds to a speed of 39 mph.

The lower quartile corresponds to 25%, which is 40. The speed is 33 mph. The upper quartile corresponds to 75%, which is 120. The speed is 44 mph.

Examination questions

1. *Given that the 'wheat' sector
in the pie chart represents 63 000 tonnes,
the number of tonnes of oats grown is
A 88 200   B 54 000   C 45 000
D 36 000   E 17 500* (LON)

Answer

Wheat angle = $360° - 120° - 100°$
$= 140°$.

So $140°$ represents 63 000 tonnes

$1°$ represents $\dfrac{63\,000}{140}$ tonnes

$100°$ represents $\dfrac{63\,000}{140} \times 100$ tonnes

$= 45\,000$ tonnes

The answer is C.

Comment

angle proportional to
amount grown

2. *The mean of the numbers 4, 8 and x is the same as the mean of the
numbers 3, 4, 6 and 7. x =*
A 3   B 5   C 6   D 8   E 12 (LON)

Answer

$$\frac{4 + 8 + x}{3} = \frac{3 + 4 + 6 + 7}{4}$$

$$\frac{12 + x}{3} = \frac{20}{4}$$

$$12 + x = 15$$

$$x = 3 \quad \text{answer A.}$$

Comment

$$\text{mean} = \frac{\text{total}}{\text{total number}}$$

3. *The bar chart illustrates the weekly expenditure of a family on rent, food and fuel. Sketch a pie chart to represent this information, marking the size of the angle in each sector.* (LON)

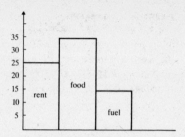

Answer

		%	angle
rent	25	33·3	120
food	35	46·7	168
fuel	15	20·0	72
total	75	100·0	360

Comment

make a table and calculate % and angle

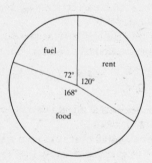

4. *Five integers have a mode of 2, a median of 3 and a mean of 4. Which of the following gives all possible values for the largest integer?*
A 7, 8 or 9   B 7 or 8 only   C 8 or 9 only   D 9 only. (AEB)

Answer Median = 3; mode = 2, so there are at least two 2s. Three of the numbers, then, must be 2, 2 and 3. The total of all the numbers is 5 × mean = 5 × 4 = 20. The total of 2, 2 and 3 is 7, so the other two numbers total 13. Since the numbers must be greater than the median, 3, then possible pairs of numbers are 9 and 4, 8 and 5 and 7 and 6. The possible values for the largest integer are 7, 8 and 9. The answer is A.

Section 16: Sets

A set is a collection of things, for example numbers or letters. The contents of the sets are called *elements*, and are enclosed in curly brackets; $\{1, 2, 3, 4, 5\}, \{a, b, c, d, e, f, g\}, \{\bigcirc, \square, \triangle, \diamond\}$.

A set is denoted by a capital letter, and its elements by small letters. The symbol $\in$ is used to show that a particular element belongs to a set, written as a∈A.

Subsets: A set of which all the elements belong to a larger set is said to be a subset of the larger set. If A is a subset of B, the notation is $A \subset B$.

Union and intersection: Two sets can be combined by taking all of their elements together. The resulting set is called the *union* of the two sets. The union of A and B is written as $A \cup B$.

The elements that belong to both of the two sets form the *intersection* of the two sets. The intersection of A and B is written as $A \cap B$.

Example If $A = \{1, 2, 3, 4, 7\}$ and $B = \{2, 4, 6, 8\}$ then $A \cup B = \{1, 2, 3, 4, 6, 7, 8\}$ and $A \cap B = \{2, 4\}$

The empty set has no elements at all, not even the number 0. It is written as $\{\ \}$, or denoted by the symbol $\varnothing$.

The universal set contains all of the elements that are involved with a particular problem. For example, if the sets contained integers between 1 and 10, then the universal set would be $\{1, 2, 3, 4, 5, 6, 7, 8, 9, 10\}$. If the problem concerned sets of letters, then the universal set would be the alphabet. The universal set is denoted by the symbol ξ.

The complement of a set contains all the elements not in the set. It is found by crossing out the elements in the set from the universal set. The complement of the set A is denoted by A'.

Example If $\xi = \{1, 2, 3, 4, 5, 6, 7, 8, 9, 10\}$ and $A = \{1, 4, 7\}$ then $A' = \{2, 3, 5, 6, 8, 9, 10\}$.

Sets can be visualized on a *Venn diagram*. Shapes which are often, but not always, circles are used to represent the sets. The elements of each set can be inserted in the appropriate places in the diagram.

Union, intersection and complement can be shown on a diagram, as can relations between sets.

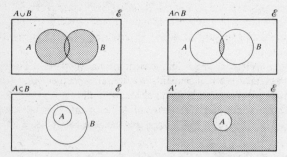

All the sets are contained in a rectangle which represents the universal set.

Example

Given that n is an integer and that $\xi = \{n : 3 \leqslant n < 16\}$, with subsets A, B and C such that A = {multiples of 3}, B = {multiples of 4} and C = {multiples of 5}, complete the Venn diagram:

Use your diagram to list the members of

(a) A   (b) B $\cup$ C   (c) B $\cap$ C
(d) $(A \cup B \cup C)'$ (AEB)

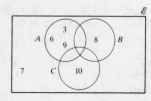

Answer The numbers are put into the diagram according to their factors; for example, 12 has factors 3 and 4, but not 5, so that 12 goes in the intersection of *A* and *B* but outside *C*.

(a) $A = 3, 6, 9, 12, 15$
(b) $B \cup C = 4, 8, 12, 5, 10, 15$
(c) $B \cap C = \varnothing$
(d) $(A \cup B \cup C)' = 7, 11, 13, 14$

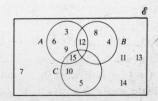

Notation summary

Capital letters denote sets; small letters denote elements.

$a \in A$ means that a is an element of A.

$A \subset B$ means that A is a subset of B – all the elements of A are in B.

$A \cup B$ is the union of A and B, containing all the elements of both A and B.

$A \cap B$ is the intersection of A and B, containing all the elements which belong to both sets.

A' is the complement of A – all the elements not in A.

ξ is the universal set – all elements involved in a problem.

$\varnothing$ is the empty set, containing no elements at all.

$n(A)$ means the number of elements of A.

Examination questions and examples

1. If $P = \{a, l, d, e, r, s, h, o, t\}$, $Q = \{m, a, t, h, s\}$ *and* $R = \{e, x, a, m, s\}$ *then* $n(P \cup Q \cup R) =$

A 4   B 11   C 14   D 19 (A E B)

Answer	**Comments**
$P \cup Q \cup R = \{a, l, d, e, r, s, h, o, t, m, x\}$	all the letters, without repetitions
So $n(P \cup Q \cup R) = 11$	number of elements
The answer is B.	

2. If $X = \{4, 6, 8, 10\}$, $Y = \{3, 6, 9\}$ *and* $Z = \{1, 2, 3, 6\}$ *then* I $(X \cap Y) \subset Z$
II $(Y \cap Z) \subset X$ III $(X \cap Z) \subset Y$

A I and II only   B I and III only   C II and III only   D I, II and III

(A E B)

Answer	**Comments**
$X \cap Y = \{6\} \subset Z$	find the intersection, is it in Z?
So I is true.	
$Y \cap Z = \{3, 6\}$ *not a subset of* X	3 is not in X
So II is false.	
$X \cap Z = \{6\} \subset Y$	
So III is true.	
I and III are true; the answer is B.	

3. The universal set consists of positive integers less than 50. $A = \{x: x \text{ is divisible by } 5\}$ and $B = \{x: 3x - 1 > 57\}$. List the elements of the set $A \cap B$.

Answer

$A = \{0, 5, 10, 15, 20, 25, 30, 35, 40, 45\}$
For the elements of B
$3x - 1 > 57$
$\quad 3x > 58$

$\quad\quad x > 19\frac{1}{3}$

x must be an integer, so
$B = \{20, 21, 22, ..., 49\}$.
$A \cap B$ is the overlap of these two sets,
and so $A \cap B = \{20, 25, 30, 35, 40, 45\}$.

Comments

divisible by 5, less than 50

add 1 over

divide by the *positive* number 3

---

4. *In a school of 2000 pupils, 1200 study history and 900 study geography. 300 study both subjects. The number who study neither is*
A 100   B 200   C 300   D 400   E 500(LON)

Answer

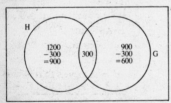

Middle = number studying both
$\quad\quad\quad = 300$
Number studying only history
$= 1200 - 300 = 900$
Number studying only geography
$= 900 - 300 = 600$
The total in the two sets is
$900 + 300 + 600 = 1800$; ξ is 2 000,
so $2000 - 1800 = 200$ study neither.
The answer is B.

Comments
Draw a diagram. Put the centre (intersection) number in first. Then work outwards. The number in each section gives the *number of elements* in that part

5. Sets are defined as follows:

$\xi = \{$cars in a certain car park$\}$

$R = \{$red cars$\}$

$F = \{$cars not made in Great Britain$\}$

$A = \{$cars with automatic transmission$\}$

$H = \{$cars with a rear door ('hatchbacks')$\}$

$M = \{$cars with engines of more than 2 litres capacity$\}$

$S = \{$cars with sun roofs$\}$

Write sentences, *NOT* using set language, to express the following statements:

(a) $F' \cap H = \varnothing$ (b) $H \cap R = H$ (c) $A \cup M = A$.

Express the following statements in set language:

(d) None of the red cars has both automatic transmission and a sun roof.

(e) Only cars made in Great Britain have engines of more than 2 litres capacity.

(f) All the cars not made in Great Britain have sun roofs. (LON)

Answer

(a) No British car has a hatchback.

(b) All hatchbacks are red.

(c) All cars with capacity of more than 2 litres are automatic.

(d) No car is red, automatic and also has a sun roof:

$$R \cap A \cap S = \varnothing$$

(e) $M \subset F'$

(f) $F \subset S$

Comments

F' is the complement of F, i.e. British cars. $F' \cap H$ is the set of British cars with hatchbacks

$A \cap B = A$ means that $A \subset B$

$A \cup B = A$ means that $B \subset A$.

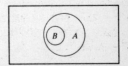

or $M \cap F = \varnothing$

or $F \cap S = F$

6. *(i) Draw a single Venn diagram to illustrate the relations between the following sets:*

P = {parallelograms},   Q = {quadrilaterals},   R = {rectangles}, S = {squares}, Z = {quadrilaterals having one and only one pair of parallel sides}.

State which one of the sets P, R, S, Z, $\varnothing$ is equal to
(a) $R \cap S$ (b) $P \cap Z$

(ii) The 89 members of the fifth form all belong to one or more of the Chess Club, the Debating Society and the Jazz Club. Denoting these sets by C, D and J respectively, it is known that 20 pupils belong to C only, 15 to J only and 12 to D only. Given that $n(C \cap J) = 18$, $n(C \cap D) = 20$ and $n(D \cap J) = 16$, calculate
(a) $n(C \cap J \cap D)$ (b) $n(D')$. (LON)

Answer

(i) $S \subset R \subset P \subset Q$

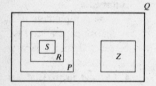

Comments

see p. 124 (quadrilaterals). A square is a rectangle. A rectangle is a parallelogram. All are quadrilaterals

(a) $R \cap S = S$
(b) $P \cap Z = \varnothing$

as S is a subset of R
parallelograms have both pairs of sides parallel

(ii)

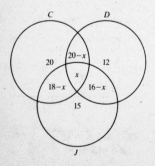

start from the middle, which is unknown so call it x, and work outwards the numbers on the diagram refer to the number of members of each subset

(a) If $n(C \cap J \cap D) = x$, then adding all the numbers together from the diagram:

$20 + 20 - x + x + 18 - x + 12 + 16 - x + 15$ the total number of pupils
$= 89$ is 89

so $\quad 101 - 2x = 89$
$\qquad\qquad 2x = 12$
$\qquad\qquad\; x = 6$
$n(C \cap J \cap D) = 6$

  (b) $n(D') = 89 - 42$ since $n(D)$
$\qquad\qquad = 47$ $= 20 - x + x + 16 - x + 12$
$\qquad\qquad\qquad$ $= 20 + 16 - x + 12 = 48 - x$
$\qquad\qquad\qquad$ $= 48 - 6 = 42$

Section 17: Symmetry

If a line cuts a figure into two mirror images, then the figure is said to have *line* or *plane* symmetry, and the line is called the axis of symmetry of the figure.

Examples

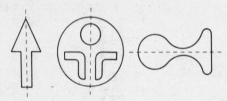

The dotted lines are the axes of symmetry. A regular polygon with *n* sides has *n* axes of symmetry.

If one half of a figure can be rotated about a point so as to fit the other half, then it is said to have *point* or *rotational* symmetry.

Examples

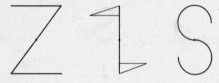

Examination questions

1. (a) The triangle ABC with AB = AC has symmetry about a line. Draw the line and mark it L

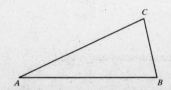

(b) From the word

HAMPSHIRE

Write down all the letters that do not have symmetry about a point or line. (A E B)

Answer

(a)

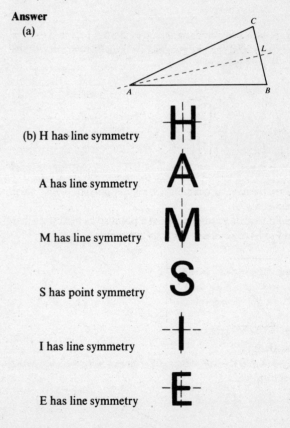

(b) H has line symmetry

A has line symmetry

M has line symmetry

S has point symmetry

I has line symmetry

E has line symmetry

The letters with no symmetry are P and R.

Section 18: Vectors and Matrices – AB, **a**, $\binom{1}{2}$, $\left(\begin{smallmatrix} 1 & 2 \\ 3 & 4 \end{smallmatrix}\right)$

Vectors

Vector is the Latin for carrier. A vector represents a *movement* from one point to another. It is pictured as an arrow.

This is the vector from A to B
it is written as $\vec{AB}$; the arrow
on top tells you that the movement is towards B. The opposite move from B to A would be written as $\vec{BA}$.

The move from A to B can be followed by a move from B to a third point C.

The combined move from A to B and then to C *corresponds* to adding the two vectors $\vec{AB}$ and $\vec{BC}$. The result is a move from A to C, that is $\vec{AC}$.

The addition can be expressed as

$$\vec{AB} + \vec{BC} = \vec{AC}$$

Any number of vectors can be added together in this way, following one movement with another.

$$\vec{XY} + \vec{YZ} + \vec{ZW} + \vec{WU} = \vec{XU}.$$

Zero vectors

The vector $\vec{AA}$ corresponds to starting and finishing at the same place, in other words no movement at all. $\vec{AA}$ is a zero vector. $\vec{BB}, \vec{CC}, \vec{DD}$ and so on are also zero vectors. The bold **0** is used for a zero vector.

Negative vectors

Following $\vec{AB}$ with $\vec{BA}$, $\vec{AB} + \vec{BA} = \vec{AA} = \mathbf{0}$ which leads to

$$\vec{BA} = -\vec{AB}.$$

Subtracting vectors can be done by *adding* negative vectors. Vectors can also be written as single bold small letters, for example $\mathbf{a} = \vec{AB}$, $\mathbf{p} = \vec{PQ}$. They can be scaled up or down by multiplying by numbers. $2\mathbf{p}$ is twice as long as $\mathbf{p}$, $3\vec{AB}$ is 3 times $\vec{AB}$. $\frac{1}{2}\vec{AB}$ points to the mid point of $\vec{AB}$.

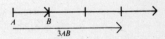

Equal vectors

The start and end points of a vector do not actually matter; what is important is the length and direction of the move. Two vectors are taken to be *equal* if they are parallel and have the same length.

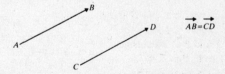

Because of this, vectors can be added even when they do not have common end points. For example
$\vec{AB} + \vec{CD} = \vec{AB} + \vec{BE} = \vec{AE}$,
where E is a point such that
$\vec{BE}$ is equal to $\vec{CD}$. In fact
$BEDC$ is a parallelogram.

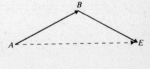

If $\vec{OA} = \mathbf{a}$ and $\vec{OB} = \mathbf{b}$, then $\vec{AB} = \vec{AO} + \vec{OB} = -\vec{AO} + \vec{OB} = -\mathbf{a} + \mathbf{b}$.
So that $\vec{AB} = \mathbf{b} - \mathbf{a}$.

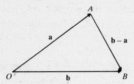

Examination questions and examples

1. In the regular hexagon $OPQRST$, $\vec{OP} = \mathbf{p}$ and $\vec{OT} = \mathbf{t}$. Express $\vec{PT}$
in terms of $\mathbf{p}$ and $\mathbf{t}$ and show that
(a) $\vec{PS} = 2\mathbf{t}$ (b) $\vec{OS} = \mathbf{p} + 2\mathbf{t}$

*   Given that $\vec{PX} = \frac{2}{3}\vec{PT}$ show that X lies on OS and find the value of*
$\frac{OX}{XS}$ (LON)

Answer

Comments

draw a diagram first
a regular hexagon has equal
sides and all interior angles
are $120°$ (see p. 126)

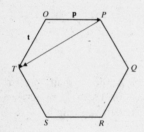

$\vec{PT} = \vec{PO} + \vec{OT}$
$\quad = -\vec{OP} + \vec{OT}$
$\quad = -\mathbf{p} + \mathbf{t}$
$\vec{PT} = \mathbf{t} - \mathbf{p}$
$\quad$ (a)

to find $\vec{PT}$, trace a route
round given vectors that
starts at P and ends at T.
$\vec{PO} = -\vec{OP}$ (see p. 187)
join the vertices up to the
centre

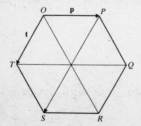

All the triangles are equilateral,
so that $PS = 2OT$ and PS is parallel
to OT. This proves that
$$\vec{PS} = 2\vec{OT} = 2\mathbf{t}$$
  (b) $\vec{OS} = \vec{OP} + \vec{PS}$ find a route from O to S

            $= \mathbf{p} + 2\mathbf{t}$

                                            draw a new diagram
                                            showing X

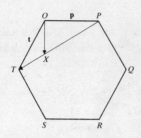

$$\vec{OX} = \vec{OP} + \vec{PX} = \mathbf{p} + \frac{2}{3}\vec{PT}$$

$$= \mathbf{p} + \frac{2}{3}(\mathbf{t} - \mathbf{p})$$

$$= \mathbf{p} + \frac{2}{3}\mathbf{t} - \frac{2}{3}\mathbf{p}$$

$$= \frac{1}{3}\mathbf{p} + \frac{2}{3}\mathbf{t}$$

$$= \frac{1}{3}(\mathbf{p} + 2\mathbf{t})$$

Also $\vec{OS} = \vec{OP} + \vec{PS}$

       $= \mathbf{p} + 2\mathbf{t}$

so $\vec{OX} = \dfrac{1}{3}\vec{OS}.$

This means that OX and OS are parallel $\vec{OX}$ is a scaled down $\vec{OS}$
But since they have the point O in
common, then X must lie on OS.

Also, since $OX = \frac{1}{3}OS$ then

$$\frac{OX}{XS} = \frac{1}{2} \qquad\qquad OX = \frac{1}{3}OS \Rightarrow XS = \frac{2}{3}OS$$

Notice that to show that a point A lies on the line BC, you show that $\vec{BA}$ is a multiple of $\vec{BC}$.

2. The diagram shows a triangle OAB and points P and Q such that $\vec{AQ} = 2\vec{QB}$ and $\vec{OP} = \vec{PB}$. $\vec{OA} = \mathbf{a}$ and $\vec{OB} = \mathbf{b}$. Express the following vectors as simply as possible in terms of $\mathbf{a}$ and $\mathbf{b}$: (i) $\vec{OQ}$ (ii) $\vec{QP}$.

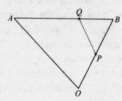

Answer

(i) $\vec{OQ} = \vec{OA} + \vec{AQ}$ route from O to Q

     $= \vec{OA} + \frac{2}{3}\vec{AB}$ Q divides AB in the ratio $2:1$

   $\vec{AB} = \vec{AO} + \vec{OB}$

       $= -\mathbf{a} + \mathbf{b}$

So $\vec{OQ} = \mathbf{a} + \frac{2}{3}(\mathbf{b} - \mathbf{a})$ putting $\mathbf{a}$ for $\vec{OA}$

       $= \mathbf{a} - \frac{2}{3}\mathbf{a} + \frac{2}{3}\mathbf{b}$

   $\vec{OQ} = \frac{1}{3}\mathbf{a} + \frac{2}{3}\mathbf{b}.$

(ii) $\vec{QP} = \vec{QO} + \vec{OP}$

     $= -\vec{OQ} + \vec{OP}$

     $= -\frac{1}{3}\mathbf{a} - \frac{2}{3}\mathbf{b} + \frac{1}{2}\mathbf{b}$

   $\vec{QP} = -\frac{1}{3}\mathbf{a} - \frac{1}{6}\mathbf{b}.$ $-\frac{2}{3} + \frac{1}{2} = -\frac{1}{6}$

Vectors and coordinates

If vectors are represented as moves on the x–y plane, then each move has a certain amount in the x-direction (x-component) and a certain amount in the y-direction (y-component) (x is left–right, and y is up–down).

This is the vector $\vec{AB}$, which
has a movement of 2 units to the
right and 3 up.

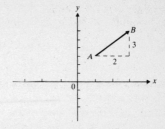

Imagine that you are playing a game on graph paper. You throw a die
once to find the move in the x-direction and once again for the move in
the y direction. The two numbers are recorded in brackets as for example
$\binom{2}{3}$, where the top number is for x and the bottom one is for y.

Starting from the origin, the object of the game is to reach a given
point on the plane by making successive moves. For each throw of the die
you can choose to take the score as $+$ or $-$. A $+$ means that you move
right or up, and a $-$ means that you move left or down. For example, the
move $\binom{-2}{4}$ is 2 *left* and 4 *up* (remember that the top number is the x
value).

Suppose that the next move is $\binom{1}{1}$. Plotting these on the board
A move of $\binom{-2}{4}$ followed
by a move of $\binom{1}{1}$
You end up at the point
$(-1, 5)$. You would end up
at the same point if you
made the single move
$\binom{-1}{5}$

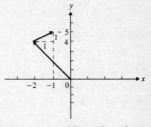

Putting this together, vectors can be represented by pairs of numbers
in brackets $\binom{1}{2}$. When adding two vectors in this form, add the numbers
separately

$$\binom{1}{2} + \binom{3}{2} = \binom{4}{4}$$

If you make the same move twice, it doubles the effect of both the x and
the y movement. This can be written as

$$2\binom{x}{y} = \binom{2x}{2y}$$

In fact, when you multiply a vector by any number, just multiply the separate numbers inside the brackets.

$$3\binom{1}{2} = \binom{3}{6} \qquad \frac{1}{2}\binom{4}{6} = \binom{2}{3} \qquad -4\binom{1}{-1} = \binom{-4}{4}$$

You may want to know the *size* of the move. This means the length of the vector. It is given the name *modulus*, and can be calculated by using Pythagoras' Theorem (see p. 108).

For example, to find the length of the move $\binom{3}{4}$:

From the right-angled triangle

$$a^2 = 3^2 + 4^2$$
$$= 9 + 16$$
$$= 25$$

so that $a = 5$ (taking square roots)

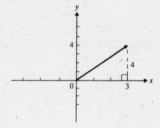

The modulus of the vector $\binom{3}{4}$ is 5.

When a vector is written in the form $\binom{3}{4}$, it is called a *column vector*.

Examples

1. Simplify $3\binom{2}{-1} + 7\binom{-1}{6}$.

Answer   **Comments**

$$3\binom{2}{-1} + 7\binom{-1}{6} = \binom{6}{-3} + \binom{-7}{42}$$ multiply the numbers inside the brackets

$$= \binom{6-7}{-3+42}$$ add the numbers separately

$$= \binom{-1}{39}.$$

2. $2\binom{t}{1+t} - 4\binom{s}{-1} = \binom{6}{0}$; calculate s and t.

Answer	**Comments**

$$\begin{pmatrix} 2t \\ 2+2t \end{pmatrix} - \begin{pmatrix} 4s \\ -4 \end{pmatrix} = \begin{pmatrix} 6 \\ 0 \end{pmatrix}$$

$$\begin{pmatrix} 2t-4s \\ 2+2t+4 \end{pmatrix} = \begin{pmatrix} 6 \\ 0 \end{pmatrix} \qquad \text{combine the vectors}$$

So $\quad t - 2s = 3$ comparing both sides and dividing
and $\quad t + 3 = 0$ by 2

The second equation gives $t = -3$.
Put this into the first:

$$\begin{aligned} -3 - 2s &= 3 \\ -2s &= 6 \qquad \text{take the } -3 \text{ over} \\ s &= -3 \qquad \text{divide by } -2 \end{aligned}$$

Matrices

A matrix is a rectangular array of numbers, enclosed in brackets. Examples:

$$\begin{pmatrix} 1 & 1 & 1 \\ 2 & 3 & 6 \end{pmatrix} \qquad \begin{pmatrix} 1 & 1 & 2 \\ 8 & 6 & 4 \\ 2 & 1 & 3 \\ 8 & 9 & 0 \end{pmatrix} \qquad \begin{pmatrix} 1 & 2 \\ 2 & 1 \end{pmatrix} \qquad \begin{pmatrix} 4 \\ 5 \end{pmatrix} \qquad (3,6)$$

A column vector is also a matrix.

If the matrix has m rows and n columns, then it is called an *m by n matrix*. We shall be concerned only with 2 by 2 matrices.

Matrices can be added and subtracted in the same way as column vectors, by adding or subtracting corresponding numbers of the two matrices:

$$\begin{pmatrix} 1 & 2 \\ 3 & 4 \end{pmatrix} + \begin{pmatrix} 2 & 1 \\ 3 & 5 \end{pmatrix} = \begin{pmatrix} 1+2 & 2+1 \\ 3+3 & 4+5 \end{pmatrix} = \begin{pmatrix} 3 & 3 \\ 6 & 9 \end{pmatrix}$$

Matrices can also be multiplied by numbers

$$2\begin{pmatrix} 1 & 2 \\ 3 & 4 \end{pmatrix} = \begin{pmatrix} 2 & 4 \\ 6 & 8 \end{pmatrix}$$

Matrix × vector multiplication

To multiply a matrix by a vector, for example $\begin{pmatrix} 1 & 2 \\ 3 & 4 \end{pmatrix}\begin{pmatrix} 1 \\ 3 \end{pmatrix}$, take the top half of the matrix, $(1 \quad 2)$, and turn it round to form a column vector $\begin{pmatrix} 1 \\ 2 \end{pmatrix}$. Multiply this vector by the vector $\begin{pmatrix} 1 \\ 3 \end{pmatrix}$ by multiplying the separate numbers and then *adding* the results.

$$\begin{pmatrix} 1 \\ 2 \end{pmatrix} \cdot \begin{pmatrix} 1 \\ 3 \end{pmatrix} = (1 \times 1) + (2 \times 3) = 7.$$

So, for the top half, $\begin{pmatrix} 1 & 2 \\ . & . \end{pmatrix}\begin{pmatrix} 1 \\ 3 \end{pmatrix} = \begin{pmatrix} 7 \\ . \end{pmatrix}$

Now repeat the process with the bottom half of the matrix:

$$(3 \quad 4) \rightarrow \begin{pmatrix} 3 \\ 4 \end{pmatrix}, \text{ multiply by } \begin{pmatrix} 1 \\ 3 \end{pmatrix}, \text{ to give } (3 \times 1) + (4 \times 3) = 15.$$

The result of the multiplication is

$$\begin{pmatrix} 1 & 2 \\ 3 & 4 \end{pmatrix}\begin{pmatrix} 1 \\ 3 \end{pmatrix} = \begin{pmatrix} 7 \\ 15 \end{pmatrix}$$

The matrix has multiplied the vector to give another vector; the vector has been *transformed.*

Transformations move points, or vectors, around the x–y plane. The result of transforming a particular object point or figure is called its image under the transformation. To see the effect of a particular transformation, it is often useful to look at the image of a simple shape under the transformation. In the examples following, the *unit square O I K J* is taken, and its images under various transformations are drawn.

The unit square has vertices at the points $O(0, 0)$, $I(1, 0)$, $K(1, 1)$ and $J(0, 1)$.

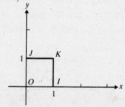

Some types of transformation

1. *Translation.* All points are moved by given amounts in the x and y

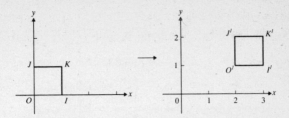

directions. For example, a translation of 2 units in the x-direction, and 1 unit in the y-direction:

Notice that this translation can be represented by the column vector $\binom{2}{1}$.

Areas and lengths are unchanged.

2. *Reflection in a given line.* The line acts as a mirror through which the points are reflected.

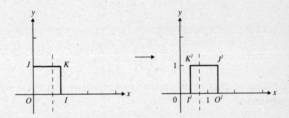

The line of the reflection is called an *invariant* line of the transformation, since the points on it are unaffected by the reflection.

Areas and lengths are unaffected by the reflection.

3. *Rotation.* The points rotate through a given angle about a given point, called the *centre of the rotation.*

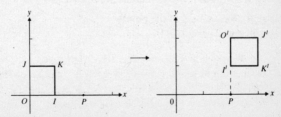

Rotation of 90° clockwise with centre P.

The centre of the rotation is invariant. Lengths and areas are unchanged.

4. *Enlargement by a given factor about a given point.* For any point P, its distance from the given point is multiplied by the given factor:

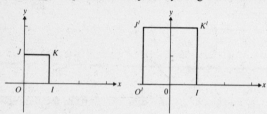

Enlargement about the point $I(1, 0)$ with scale factor 2.

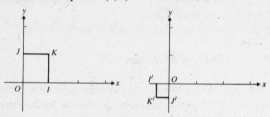

Enlargement about the point $O(0, 0)$ with scale factor $-\frac{1}{2}$. When the factor is negative, the directions are reversed.

The given point for the enlargement is invariant. The image is *similar* to the object, so that if the lengths are multiplied by 2, for example, then the areas are multiplied by $2^2 = 4$ (see p. 124).

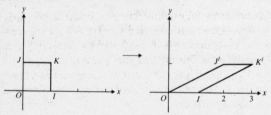

5. *Shear in the direction of a given line.* Points are moved parallel to the given line, by an amount which is proportional to the distance of the point from the given line.

Shear in the direction of the x-axis. y is unchanged, but x changes according to the rule $x \rightarrow x + 2y$. The square has been pushed over to form a parallelogram which has the same area. The given line, in this case the x-axis, is the invariant line of the shear.

More complicated transformations can be made by combining any of these: for example, a rotation followed by a reflection:

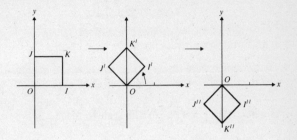

Transformations and Matrices

As you saw on p. 194, a matrix can represent a transformation. To find the image of a given point, multiply the matrix by the corresponding column vector. The effect of the transformation can be seen by multiplying the vectors $\binom{0}{0}$, $\binom{1}{0}$, $\binom{1}{1}$ and $\binom{0}{1}$, which correspond to the vertices of the unit square.

Draw the square and its image in the x–y plane, and compare with the transformations listed above.

Other simple figures, for example triangles, could equally well be used to show the effect of the transformation. Conversely, given a transformation which leaves the origin $O(0, 0)$ *unaffected* (*or invariant*), *you can find a* matrix to represent it. The method goes like this:

Suppose that the images of the points $I(1, 0)$ and $J(0, 1)$ are (p, q) and (r, s) respectively. This can be expressed in a notation similar to that used for functions (see p. 67) as

$$T: (1,0) \to (p, q)$$
$$T: (0, 1) \to (r, s) \text{ where } T \text{ is the name of the transformation.}$$

Then the matrix which represents the transformation T is $\left(\begin{smallmatrix} p & r \\ q & s \end{smallmatrix}\right)$.

You can check that this is correct by multiplying this matrix with $\binom{1}{0}$ and $\binom{0}{1}$ to see that you get images $\binom{p}{q}$ and $\binom{r}{s}$.

Example Consider the transformation represented by

$$T:\begin{pmatrix} x \\ y \end{pmatrix} \rightarrow \begin{pmatrix} 1 & 3 \\ 0 & 1 \end{pmatrix}\begin{pmatrix} x \\ y \end{pmatrix}$$

First, find the image of the rectangle with vertices $O(0, 0)$, $A(4, 0)$, $B(4, 2)$ and $C(0, 2)$ under this transformation.

Multiply the column vectors representing the vertices of the rectangle by the matrix of the transformation, using the method of p. 194:

$$O\begin{pmatrix} 1 & 3 \\ 0 & 1 \end{pmatrix}\begin{pmatrix} 0 \\ 0 \end{pmatrix} = \begin{pmatrix} 0 \\ 0 \end{pmatrix} \qquad A\begin{pmatrix} 1 & 3 \\ 0 & 1 \end{pmatrix}\begin{pmatrix} 4 \\ 0 \end{pmatrix} = \begin{pmatrix} 4 \\ 0 \end{pmatrix}$$

$$B\begin{pmatrix} 1 & 3 \\ 0 & 1 \end{pmatrix}\begin{pmatrix} 4 \\ 2 \end{pmatrix} = \begin{pmatrix} 10 \\ 2 \end{pmatrix} \qquad C\begin{pmatrix} 1 & 3 \\ 0 & 1 \end{pmatrix}\begin{pmatrix} 0 \\ 2 \end{pmatrix} = \begin{pmatrix} 6 \\ 2 \end{pmatrix}$$

O is unchanged, $A \rightarrow A'(4, 0)$ is also unchanged, $B \rightarrow B'(10, 2)$ and $C \rightarrow C'(6, 2)$. The image is shown on the diagram below:

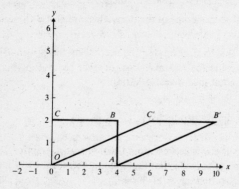

$OA'B'C'$ is a parallelogram and has the same base and height as the rectangle $OABC$. They have the same area which is $4 \times 2 = 8$ square units.

The transformation is a *shear*, with invariant line $y = 0$. The rectangle has been sheared by a factor of 3; that is, the x-coordinate is increased by three times the y-coordinate.

Remember that a shear preserves areas (see p. 196) as shown by the area calculation above.

The transformation $T:OABC \rightarrow OA'B'C'$ is represented by the matrix $\begin{pmatrix} 1 & 3 \\ 0 & 1 \end{pmatrix}$. We can ask what matrix represents the *inverse* transformation which takes $OA'B'C'$ back to $OABC$.

The inverse of a transformation takes all points back to where they started. There is a formula for the inverse of a matrix:

The inverse of the matrix $\begin{pmatrix} a & b \\ c & d \end{pmatrix}$ is $\dfrac{1}{ad-bc}\begin{pmatrix} d & -b \\ -c & a \end{pmatrix}$

To find the inverse of the matrix $\begin{pmatrix} 1 & 3 \\ 0 & 1 \end{pmatrix}$, with $a = 1$, $b = 3$, $c = 0$ and $d = 1$, we can use the formula:

$$\frac{1}{1-0}\begin{pmatrix} 1 & -3 \\ 0 & 1 \end{pmatrix} = \begin{pmatrix} 1 & -3 \\ 0 & 1 \end{pmatrix}$$

which is also a shear, this time with factor -3.

We can also find the image of the parallelogram $OA'B'C'$ under a further transformation $\begin{pmatrix} 1 & 2 \\ 0 & 1 \end{pmatrix}$.

We could do this by multiplying the vectors by the new matrix. Another way is to combine the two matrices together by multiplying, to get the matrix of the combined transformation.

The matrix $\times$ matrix product is $\begin{pmatrix} 1 & 2 \\ 0 & 1 \end{pmatrix}\begin{pmatrix} 1 & 3 \\ 0 & 1 \end{pmatrix}$.

Notice that the matrix representing the first transformation is put on the right, since this is the side that the column vectors are put (compare the method with functions, p. 67).

Matrices can be multiplied by splitting the second one into column vectors, and then using the rule for multiplying matrices and vectors of p. 194.

So $\qquad \begin{pmatrix} 1 & 2 \\ 0 & 1 \end{pmatrix}\begin{pmatrix} 1 & 3 \\ 0 & 1 \end{pmatrix} = \begin{pmatrix} 1 & 2 \\ 0 & 1 \end{pmatrix}\begin{pmatrix} 1 & 3 \\ 0 & 1 \end{pmatrix} = \begin{pmatrix} 1 & 5 \\ 0 & 1 \end{pmatrix}$

since $\begin{pmatrix} 1 & 2 \\ 0 & 1 \end{pmatrix}\begin{pmatrix} 1 \\ 0 \end{pmatrix} = \begin{pmatrix} 1 \\ 0 \end{pmatrix}$ and $\begin{pmatrix} 1 & 2 \\ 0 & 1 \end{pmatrix}\begin{pmatrix} 3 \\ 1 \end{pmatrix} = \begin{pmatrix} 2+3 \\ 1 \end{pmatrix} = \begin{pmatrix} 5 \\ 1 \end{pmatrix}$.

Notice that the two shear matrices have been multiplied together and have formed a matrix which also represents a shear.

NOTE: The order in which matrices are multiplied is important. If **A** and **B** are matrices, then $\mathbf{AB} \neq \mathbf{BA}$ (as for functions, p. 70).

Some more examples of manipulating matrices follow:

Examination questions

1. $\begin{pmatrix} 2 & 3 \\ 0 & 4 \end{pmatrix}\begin{pmatrix} 1 & 5 \\ 4 & -2 \end{pmatrix} =$

$A\begin{pmatrix} 2 & 23 \\ 8 & 4 \end{pmatrix}$ $B\begin{pmatrix} 14 & 4 \\ 16 & -8 \end{pmatrix}$ $C\begin{pmatrix} 2 & 15 \\ 0 & -8 \end{pmatrix}$ $D\begin{pmatrix} 17 & 4 \\ 0 & -8 \end{pmatrix}$ $E\begin{pmatrix} 3 & 8 \\ 4 & 2 \end{pmatrix}$ (LON)

Answer $\begin{pmatrix} 2 & 3 \\ 0 & 4 \end{pmatrix}\begin{pmatrix} 1 & 5 \\ 4 & -2 \end{pmatrix} = \begin{pmatrix} 2+12 & 10-6 \\ 0+16 & 0-8 \end{pmatrix}$

$$= \begin{pmatrix} 14 & 4 \\ 16 & -8 \end{pmatrix} \text{ answer B.}$$

2. Given that $P = \begin{pmatrix} 3 & 4 \\ -2 & 1 \end{pmatrix}$ and $Q = \begin{pmatrix} 1 & 1 \\ 1 & 0 \end{pmatrix}$ then $P + 2Q =$

$A\begin{pmatrix} 4 & 6 \\ 0 & 1 \end{pmatrix}$ $B\begin{pmatrix} 4 & 5 \\ -1 & 1 \end{pmatrix}$ $C\begin{pmatrix} 7 & 9 \\ -3 & 2 \end{pmatrix}$ $D\begin{pmatrix} 5 & 6 \\ 0 & 1 \end{pmatrix}$ $E\begin{pmatrix} 5 & 6 \\ 1 & 0 \end{pmatrix}$ (LON)

Answer $\begin{pmatrix} 3 & 4 \\ -2 & 1 \end{pmatrix} + 2\begin{pmatrix} 1 & 1 \\ 1 & 0 \end{pmatrix} = \begin{pmatrix} 3+2 & 4+2 \\ -2+2 & 1+0 \end{pmatrix}$

$$= \begin{pmatrix} 5 & 6 \\ 0 & 1 \end{pmatrix}$$

The answer is D.

3. The inverse of the matrix $\begin{pmatrix} 4 & 3 \\ 6 & 5 \end{pmatrix}$ is

$A\begin{pmatrix} -5 & 3 \\ 6 & -4 \end{pmatrix}$ $B\begin{pmatrix} 5 & -3 \\ -6 & 4 \end{pmatrix}$ $C\frac{1}{2}\begin{pmatrix} -4 & 6 \\ 3 & -5 \end{pmatrix}$

$D\frac{1}{2}\begin{pmatrix} 5 & -3 \\ -6 & 4 \end{pmatrix}$ $E\frac{1}{2}\begin{pmatrix} 5 & -6 \\ -3 & 4 \end{pmatrix}$ (LON)

Answer

$a = 4$, $b = 3$, $c = 6$ and $d = 5$. $ad - bc = 20 - 18$, so by the formula the inverse is $\dfrac{1}{2}\begin{pmatrix} 5 & -3 \\ -6 & 4 \end{pmatrix}$: answer D.

Question 2 above involved the use of capital letters to represent matrices. Also, if $\mathbf{A}$ is a matrix, then its inverse is written as $\mathbf{A}^{-1}$. It is possible to have powers of matrices, for example $\mathbf{A}^2$ means $\mathbf{AA}$, multiply the matrix $\mathbf{A}$ by itself. Do not make the mistake of just squaring the numbers inside the matrix!

Example

Given that $\mathbf{M} = \begin{pmatrix} 3 & 4 \\ -1 & 0 \end{pmatrix}$, find the matrices $\mathbf{M}^2$ and $\mathbf{M}^3$.

Answer $\mathbf{M}^2 = \mathbf{MM} = \begin{pmatrix} 3 & 4 \\ -1 & 0 \end{pmatrix}\begin{pmatrix} 3 & 4 \\ -1 & 0 \end{pmatrix}$

$$= \begin{pmatrix} 3 & 4 \\ -1 & 0 \end{pmatrix}\begin{pmatrix} 3 & 4 \\ -1 & 0 \end{pmatrix}$$

$$= \begin{pmatrix} 9-4 & 12+0 \\ -3+0 & -4+0 \end{pmatrix} = \begin{pmatrix} 5 & 12 \\ -3 & -4 \end{pmatrix}$$

$$\mathbf{M}^3 = \mathbf{MM}^2 = \begin{pmatrix} 3 & 4 \\ -1 & 0 \end{pmatrix}\begin{pmatrix} 5 & 12 \\ -3 & -4 \end{pmatrix} = \begin{pmatrix} 3 & 4 \\ -1 & 0 \end{pmatrix}\begin{pmatrix} 5 & 12 \\ -3 & -4 \end{pmatrix}$$

$$= \begin{pmatrix} 15-12 & 36-16 \\ -5+0 & -12+0 \end{pmatrix} = \begin{pmatrix} 3 & 20 \\ -5 & -12 \end{pmatrix}$$

The identity matrix is the special matrix $\begin{pmatrix} 1 & 0 \\ 0 & 1 \end{pmatrix}$. It represents the identity transformation, which does nothing at all. Vectors are unaffected when multiplied by this matrix:

$$\begin{pmatrix} 1 & 0 \\ 0 & 1 \end{pmatrix}\begin{pmatrix} x \\ y \end{pmatrix} = \begin{pmatrix} x \\ y \end{pmatrix}$$

Since matrix multiplication is also defined in terms of vectors it follows that when the identity matrix multiplies another matrix it has no effect. The identity matrix is often shown as the letter $\mathbf{I}$.

An important result is that when you multiply a matrix by its inverse, the result is the identity matrix **I**. This is because the matrix and its inverse cancel each other out.

Example
$$\begin{pmatrix} 1 & -3 \\ 0 & 1 \end{pmatrix}\begin{pmatrix} 1 & 3 \\ 0 & 1 \end{pmatrix} = \begin{pmatrix} 1 & -3 \\ 0 & 1 \end{pmatrix}\begin{pmatrix} 1 \\ 0 \end{pmatrix}\begin{pmatrix} 3 \\ 1 \end{pmatrix}$$

$$= \begin{pmatrix} 1+0 & 3-3 \\ 0+0 & 0+1 \end{pmatrix}$$

$$= \begin{pmatrix} 1 & 0 \\ 0 & 1 \end{pmatrix}$$

Determinants

When finding the inverse of the matrix $\begin{pmatrix} a & b \\ c & d \end{pmatrix}$, you have to calculate the quantity $ad - bc$. This is called the *determinant* of the matrix. Notice that if the determinant is zero, then you cannot divide by the quantity $ad - bc$, and so the matrix has no inverse. A matrix that has no inverse is said to be *singular*.

Many transformations have the effect of multiplying areas by a certain factor; this factor is given by the determinant of the matrix. For example, the transformation represented by the matrix $\begin{pmatrix} 1 & 4 \\ 1 & 7 \end{pmatrix}$ scales areas by a factor of 3, since the determinant is $(1 \times 7) - (1 \times 4) = 3$.

Matrices and Simultaneous Equations

The simultaneous equations $2x + 3y = 6$
$$x - 2y = 4$$
can be written in matrix form as $\begin{pmatrix} 2 & 3 \\ 1 & -2 \end{pmatrix}\begin{pmatrix} x \\ y \end{pmatrix} = \begin{pmatrix} 6 \\ 4 \end{pmatrix}$ where the matrix is formed by the coefficients of the equations.

Multiply both sides of this matrix equation by the inverse of $\begin{pmatrix} 2 & 3 \\ 1 & -2 \end{pmatrix}$, which is found to be $\begin{pmatrix} 2/7 & 3/7 \\ 1/7 & -2/7 \end{pmatrix}$ from the formula of p. 199.

$$\begin{pmatrix} 2/7 & 3/7 \\ 1/7 & -2/7 \end{pmatrix}\begin{pmatrix} 2 & 3 \\ 1 & -2 \end{pmatrix}\begin{pmatrix} x \\ y \end{pmatrix} = \begin{pmatrix} 2/7 & 3/7 \\ 1/7 & -2/7 \end{pmatrix}\begin{pmatrix} 6 \\ 4 \end{pmatrix}$$

but matrix × inverse = identity

$$\begin{pmatrix} 1 & 0 \\ 0 & 1 \end{pmatrix}\begin{pmatrix} x \\ y \end{pmatrix} = \begin{pmatrix} 2/7 & 3/7 \\ 1/7 & -2/7 \end{pmatrix}\begin{pmatrix} 6 \\ 4 \end{pmatrix}$$

so
$$\begin{pmatrix} x \\ y \end{pmatrix} = \begin{pmatrix} 24/7 \\ -2/7 \end{pmatrix}$$

when the multiplications are performed.

So the solution of the equations is $x = \frac{24}{7}$, $y = -\frac{2}{7}$.

$m \times n$ matrices

As mentioned at the start of the section, there are other types of matrix. They also can be added, subtracted and multiplied. A matrix that has m rows and n columns is said to be an $m \times n$ matrix.

Two matrices can only be added or subtracted if they have the same number of rows and the same number of columns.

$(m \times n) + (m \times n)$ gives $m \times n$

Example
$$\begin{pmatrix} 1 & 2 & 3 \\ 4 & 5 & 6 \end{pmatrix} + \begin{pmatrix} 1 & 0 & 1 \\ 2 & 1 & 5 \end{pmatrix} = \begin{pmatrix} 1+1 & 2+0 & 3+1 \\ 4+2 & 5+1 & 6+5 \end{pmatrix}$$
$$= \begin{pmatrix} 2 & 2 & 4 \\ 6 & 6 & 11 \end{pmatrix}$$

Two matrices can only be multiplied when the number of columns of the first one is the same as the number of rows of the second one.

$$m \times n \text{ times } n \times p \text{ gives } m \times p$$

Example

$$\begin{pmatrix} 1 & 2 & 3 \\ 4 & 1 & 5 \end{pmatrix} \begin{pmatrix} 3 & 1 \\ 2 & 1 \\ 1 & 1 \end{pmatrix} = \begin{pmatrix} 1 & 2 & 3 \\ 4 & 1 & 5 \end{pmatrix} \begin{pmatrix} 3 \\ 2 \\ 1 \end{pmatrix} \begin{pmatrix} 1 \\ 1 \\ 1 \end{pmatrix}$$

$$= \begin{pmatrix} 3 \times 1 + 2 \times 2 + 3 \times 1 & 1 \times 1 + 2 \times 1 + 3 \times 1 \\ 4 \times 3 + 1 \times 2 + 5 \times 1 & 4 \times 1 + 1 \times 1 + 5 \times 1 \end{pmatrix}$$

$$= \begin{pmatrix} 10 & 6 \\ 19 & 10 \end{pmatrix}$$

Matrices which have the same number of rows as columns are called *square matrices*. There is an identity matrix for each size of square matrix.

$\begin{pmatrix} 1 & 0 \\ 0 & 1 \end{pmatrix}$ for 2 × 2, $\begin{pmatrix} 1 & 0 & 0 \\ 0 & 1 & 0 \\ 0 & 0 & 1 \end{pmatrix}$ for 3 × 3, and so on.

Matrices such as $\begin{pmatrix} 0 & 0 \\ 0 & 0 \end{pmatrix}$ and $\begin{pmatrix} 0 & 0 & 0 \\ 0 & 0 & 0 \\ 0 & 0 & 0 \end{pmatrix}$ where all the numbers are 0s, are said to be *null matrices*.

Section 19: More about Numbers

Operations and Number Systems

When first learning about arithmetic, you probably came across multiplication tables. The table for multiplication by numbers up to 5 is

x	1	2	3	4	5
1	1	2	3	4	5
2	2	4	6	8	10
3	3	6	9	12	15
4	4	8	12	16	20
5	5	10	15	20	25

To multiply, for example, 3 by 4, take the number in the 3rd row and 4th column. This is 12.

Ordinary multiplication is only one way of combining two numbers together. Multiplication corresponds to finding the area of a rectangle; for example a 3 by 4 rectangle has area $3 \times 4 = 12$.

If you take the perimeter instead of the area, you get a different kind of combination. Sides a and b give a perimeter of $2(a + b)$ (see p. 108).

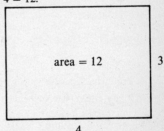

A rule for combining two numbers together to form a third is called an *operation*. (Compare with a function, which produces a number from just one number.) The operation is usually denoted with a *, so that $a*b$ would be the result of combining a and b.

For the perimeter operation above, $a*b = 2(a + b)$, and has a table

*	1	2	3	4	5
1	4	6	8	10	12
2	6	8	10	12	14
3	8	10	12	14	16
4	10	12	14	16	18
5	12	14	16	18	20

Other objects apart from numbers can have operations applied to them. For example matrices can be multiplied together (see p. 199) and functions can be combined together (see p. 69). In general an operation can be defined on any set of elements.

An operation involves:

(i) Specifying the set to be operated on.

(ii) Specifying a rule for combining members of the set.

(iii) Making a table.

* operations have some of the features of ordinary multiplication, but not always all. When numbers are multiplied in the usual way, it does not matter what order they are multiplied in. However, when matrices are multiplied the order is important. When the order can be reversed without changing the result, so that $a*b = b*a$ for all a and b in the set, then the operation is said to be *commutative* or *symmetric*.

Another property of ordinary number multiplication is *associativity*. This means that for any numbers x, y and z, $x(yz) = (xy)z$. Either pair of numbers can be multiplied first.

A general * operation is *associative* if $a*(b*c) = (a*b)*c$ for all elements in the set.

Example Let * be defined on the set of real numbers by

$$a*b = a^2 + b^2 + 4.$$

(i) Give a numerical example to show that * is commutative.

(ii) Give a numerical example to show that * is not associative.

Answer (i) Let $a = 1$ and $b = 2$,

then $1*2 = 1^2 + 2^2 + 4$

$= 1 + 4 + 4$

$= 9$

And $2*1 = 2^2 + 1^1 + 4$

$= 4 + 1 + 4$

$= 9$

So $1 * 2 = 2 * 1$; therefore * is commutative.

(ii) Let $a = 1, b = 2$ and $c = 3$.

$$1 * (2 * 3) = 1 * (2^2 + 3^2 + 4)$$
$$= 1 * (4 + 9 + 4)$$
$$= 1 * 17$$
$$= 1 + 289 + 4 = 294$$

While $\quad (1 * 2) * 3 = (1^2 + 2^2 + 4) * 3$
$$= (1 + 4 + 4) * 3$$
$$= 9 * 3 = 9^2 + 3^2 + 4$$
$$= 81 + 9 + 4 = 94$$

$1 * (2 * 3) \neq (1 * 2) * 3$; therefore * is not associative.

Identities

The number 1 has a special role in number multiplication; it has no effect on other numbers. Such an element is called an *identity*. If e is an identity for the operation *, then $e * a = a$ and $a * e = a$ for any element a. For example,

For $+$ on the real numbers, 0 is the identity.

For matrix multiplication, $\begin{pmatrix} 1 & 0 \\ 0 & 1 \end{pmatrix}$ is the identity (see p. 201).

If you have the operation table, then the identity is easy to spot. Look for the row that repeats the top row of the table exactly. The element that this row corresponds to is the identity.

Examples

1. Find the identity element from the table

*	a	b	c	d	e
a	e	a	d	b	c
b	a	b	c	d	e
c	d	c	a	e	b
d	b	d	e	d	a
e	c	e	b	a	d

Answer

The b row is $a\,b\,c\,d\,e$ which repeats the top row exactly; also the b column repeats the first column exactly. b is the identity.

2. In the operation table shown, what is the identity element?
A p   B q   C r   D s   E *there is no identity.* (LON)

*	p	q	r	s
p	r	q	p	s
q	q	p	q	p
r	p	q	s	r
s	s	p	r	s

Answer None of the rows repeats the top, so there is no identity. The answer is E. This shows that there need not be any identity element.

For number multiplication, the reciprocal of a number cancels it out leaving just 1. For example $2 \times \frac{1}{2} = 1$. For a general operation, if the element b is such that $b * a =$ identity, then b is said to be the *inverse* of a, written as a^{-1} (see p. 202, inverse matrices).

Inverses can only exist if there is an identity. To find inverses, the table can be used. For example, in the table of example 1 above, to find the inverse of c look along the c row until you find the identity element b. This occurs in the e column, so that e is the inverse of c.

Modulo Arithmetic

If n is a positive integer then the value of a number *modulo n* is the remainder after division by n. For example $3 = 1$ modulo 2, $16 = 2$ modulo 7.

The possible remainders on division by n are $0, 1, 2, 3, \ldots, n-1$. Modulo arithmetic can be used to construct new operations.

Example If * acts on the set $\{0, 1, 2, 3, 4\}$ by $a * b = ab$ modulo 5, then the operation table is

*	0	1	2	3	4
0	0	0	0	0	0
1	0	1	2	3	4
2	0	2	4	1	3
3	0	3	1	4	2
4	0	4	3	2	1

The identity is 1.

Tables can be used to solve equations; for example, we can use the modulo 5 table above to solve $3 * x = 2$. Look along the 3 row until you come across a 2. This is in the 4 column, so that the solution is $x = 4$.

Example *In modulo 12, $5 - 7 =$*
A 0   B 2   C 8   D 10 (A E B)

Answer
Ordinary addition and subtraction can be pictured on a number line. Modulo addition and subtraction can be pictured on a clock face. The numbers start at 0, and then increase round the clock to 11. Numbers greater than 11 progress round the clock more times, so that 12 corresponds to 0, 13 to 1 and so on. Addition corresponds to going round clockwise, subtraction to going round anti-clockwise.

So $5 - 7$ means start at 5 and then go round 7 positions anti-clockwise. The answer is 10, which is answer D.

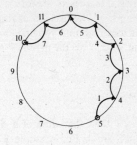

Number Bases

The position of a digit in a number determines whether it counts 1s, tens, hundreds, thousands and so on.

$$123 = 1 \times 100 + 2 \times 10 + 3 \times 1.$$

This can be written in terms of powers of ten

$$123 = 1 \times 10^2 + 2 \times 10^1 + 3 \times 1$$

Our number system has *base ten*. Other bases are possible; base 2 in particular is very important in computing. A number in base 8, for example, would be written as 123_8, the subscript 8 telling you that the base is 8. To find what this number is in the usual base ten, write it in full as

$$123_8 = 1 \times 8^2 + 2 \times 8^1 + 3 \times 1$$
$$= 1 \times 64 + 2 \times 8 + 3 \times 1$$
$$= 64 + 16 + 3$$
$$= 83 \text{ in base ten.}$$

A number in base ten can use all the digits 0, 1, 2, 3, 4, 5, 6, 7, 8 and 9; however, a number in base 8 can only use the digits 0, 1, 2, 3, 4, 5, 6 and 7. The number 8 in base 8 is written as 10_8.

Some other bases

$$315_6 = 3 \times 6^2 + 1 \times 6 + 5 \times 1 = 3 \times 36 + 6 + 5 = 119 \text{ in base ten}$$

$$1\,012_3 = 1 \times 3^3 + 0 \times 3^2 + 1 \times 3^1 + 2 \times 1 = 27 + 0 + 3 + 2$$
$$= 32 \text{ in base ten}$$

$$11\,011_2 = 1 \times 2^4 + 1 \times 2^3 + 0 \times 2^2 + 1 \times 2^1 + 1 \times 1$$
$$= 16 + 8 + 0 + 2 + 1$$
$$= 27 \text{ in base ten.}$$

Numbers in base 2 are called *binary numbers.*
Numbers in base ten are called *denary numbers.*
Numbers are converted from base ten into another base by repeatedly dividing by the new base and taking the remainders. It goes like this:

Example Convert 358 from base ten into base 8.

Answer 8)358
            8)44   remainder 6 ↑
             8)5   remainder 4
              0   remainder 5

When the number has reached 0, the remainders are read off *upwards* to give the number in base 8. The answer is 546.
   Check: $5 \times 8^2 + 4 \times 8 + 6 = 320 + 32 + 6 = 358$.

To convert from one base to another, it is usually safest to convert first of all into base ten, and then from base ten into the new base.
   Arithmetic can be done without resorting to base ten,

$$\begin{array}{r} 1\,011_2 \\ 101_2 \; + \\ \hline 10\,000_2 \\ \hline \end{array}$$ remember that 2s are carried (2 = 0 carry 1)

$$3\,125_6$$
$$121_6 \ -$$

$$3\,004_6$$

$$101_2$$
$$11_2 \ \times$$

$$101$$
$$1\,010$$

$$1\,111_2$$

Examination questions

1. Which of the following numbers are even?
I 112₃   II 122₃   III 211₃
A I and II only   B I and III only   C II and III only   D I, II and III
(AEB)

Answer	Comments
$112_3 = 1 \times 3^2 + 1 \times 3 + 2 \times 1$	convert into base ten
$\quad = 9 + 3 + 2 = 14$	which is even
$122_3 = 1 \times 3^2 + 2 \times 3 + 2 \times 1$	
$\quad = 9 + 6 + 2$	
$\quad = 17$	which is odd
$211_3 = 2 \times 3^2 + 1 \times 3 + 1 \times 1$	
$\quad = 18 + 3 + 1$	
$\quad = 22$	which is even

I and III are even, the answer is B.

2. Calculate, leaving your answer in base 8
(i) 16₈ + 14₈   (ii) 35₈ − 16₈ (AEB)

Answer

(i) 16_8 (ii) $\overset{2}{3}\overset{1}{5}_8$

$\underline{14_8} \ +$ $\underline{16_8} \ -$

32_8 17_8

Comments

$6 + 4 = \text{ten} = 12_8$

in the subtraction, borrow 8 from the 3. $15_8 = 13_{10}$

3. *When expressed in binary notation, the denary number 47 is*
A *101011* B *101111* C *110111* D *101101* (A E B)

Answer   **Comments**

2)47
2)23   rem 1
2)11   rem 1   divide and take remainders
2)5   rem 1   backwards
2)2   rem 1
2)1   rem 0
0   rem 1

The answer is 101111 which is B.

Inverse Functions

Combining functions can be thought of as an operation on the set of all functions. $f*g$ is then the function fg (see p. 69) and the *identity function* is defined by $I: x \to x$, where I stands for Identity.

When the identity function is combined with any other function it has no effect: $I(f(x)) = f(x)$ and $f(I(x)) = f(x)$.
The graph of the identity function is

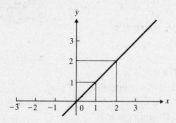

The *inverse* of a function reverses it. If, for example, $f: 2 \to 4$, then the inverse is $f^{-1}: 4 \to 2$. The result of combining a function with its inverse is the identity function. This is very similar to the idea of inverse matrices (see p. 199).

To find the inverse of a function

To find the inverse of the function $f: x \to x^2 - 3$, with domain $\{x : x \geqslant 0\}$:

Draw a flow diagram of the function, and then reverse it as when rearranging formulae (see p. 47):

$$f: x \rightarrow \boxed{\text{square}} \rightarrow \boxed{-3} \rightarrow$$

$$\leftarrow \boxed{\sqrt{}} \leftarrow \boxed{+3} \leftarrow x: f^{-1}$$

So $f^{-1}: x \rightarrow \sqrt{x+3}$. Note that the function has an inverse when x is restricted to be positive, so that $\sqrt{x}$ has only one value.

The reverse flow method cannot always be used, when x appears twice for example:

$$f: x \rightarrow \frac{1+x}{1-x}$$

The procedure is (i) label the formula as the variable y
(ii) rearrange the formula to get x in terms of y

So $\qquad\qquad y = \dfrac{1+x}{1-x}$

$\qquad y(1-x) = 1 + x \qquad\qquad$ multiply $1 - x$ across

$\qquad y - xy = 1 + x$

$\qquad y - 1 = x + xy \qquad\qquad$ move x terms across
$\qquad\qquad\qquad\qquad\qquad\qquad$ factorize
$\qquad y - 1 = x(1 + y)$

$\qquad \dfrac{y-1}{y+1} = x$

Now put the formula for x equal to $f^{-1}(y)$

$$f^{-1}(y) = \frac{y-1}{y+1}$$

Finally, since a function is usually given in terms of x, change all the ys into xs

$$f^{-1}(x) = \frac{x-1}{x+1} \text{ is the inverse function.}$$

To find the inverse of $f: x \rightarrow \log x$, use antilog. You can either use antilog tables, or press INV then LOG on a calculator.

Example

If $f(x) = \log x$, then $f^{-1}(3) = 1\,000$ (from tables or calculator).

Table of some functions and their inverses

function	inverse
$x^2 (x \geqslant 0)$	$\sqrt{x}$
$\sqrt{x}$	x^2
$\frac{1}{x}$	$\frac{1}{x}$
$2x$	$\frac{1}{2}x$
$x + 5$	$x - 5$
$5 - x$	$5 - x$
multiply x by a	divide x by a
add a to x	subtract a from x

Section 20: Probability: Calculating Risks and Chances

When tossing a fair coin, there are two possible outcomes. Either the coin shows heads or it shows tails. The chances of a head are then 1 in 2, or $\frac{1}{2}$.

The outcome of heads is called an *event*, and the chances are called the *probability* of the event. The probability of the event 'the coin shows heads' is $\frac{1}{2}$. The probability that it shows a tail is also $\frac{1}{2}$, which is why the coin is said to be fair.

Any possible outcome of an experiment or trial is called an event. The probability that the event happens is defined by the formula

$$\text{probability} = \frac{\text{number of ways the event can happen}}{\text{number of all possible outcomes}}$$

For example: A number is to be chosen at random from the numbers 1, 2, 3, 4, 5, 6, 7, 8, 9. The probability that it is even is

$$\frac{\text{number of even numbers}}{\text{number of possible numbers}} = \frac{4}{9}$$

Events are denoted by capital letters, like sets, and the probability that A happens is written as $p(A)$.

Sometimes we are interested in the possibility of more than one event happening. If two events are denoted by A and B, then the compound event 'A or B' can be formed.

For example, if A is the event 'it is raining', and B is the event 'it is cold but dry', then A or B is the event 'it is either raining or cold and dry'. A or B is often written as $A \cup B$ (see p. 177).

To find the probability of the event A or B, add the separate probabilities of A and B. In symbols

$$p(A \cup B) = p(A) + p(B)$$

(provided that A and B cannot both occur at the same time).

It may be possible that we are interested in the case when two events *both* happen. For example, if A is the event that you get a head on one throw of a coin, and B is the event that you get a head on a further throw, then $A \cap B$ is the event that you get heads both times. To find the probability of the event A and B, multiply the separate probabilities

$$p(A \cap B) = p(A)p(B)$$

(provided that A and B do not affect each other, said to be independent events).

Some other rules for handling probabilities are:

(i) The sum of the probabilities of all possible events is 1.

(ii) A probability is a number between 0 and 1; if $p(A) = 0$, then A cannot happen. If $p(A) = 1$, then A is bound to happen.

(iii) The probability that A does *not* happen is $1 - p(A)$.

It is often useful to make a list of all possible outcomes for a particular problem. This list is called the 'possibility space'.

Examination questions and examples

1. The probability that a number chosen at random from the numbers 5, 5, 5, 8, 8, 11, 11, 11 will be the mean of these numbers is
$A \frac{1}{8}$ $B \frac{1}{4}$ $C \frac{1}{3}$ $D \frac{5}{8}$ $E \frac{2}{3}$ (LON)

Answer

First the mean must be calculated (see p. 171). This is $\frac{5 + 5 + 5 + 8 + 8 + 11 + 11 + 11}{8}$ $= 8$. The probability that the number is 8 is $\frac{\text{number of 8s}}{\text{number of numbers}} = \frac{2}{8} = \frac{1}{4}$, the answer is **B**.

Comments

to say that the numbers are chosen at random means that they are all equally likely

2. Four boys each in turn toss a coin. What is the probability that the fourth boy will toss 'heads'?
$A \frac{1}{2}$ $B \frac{1}{4}$ $C \frac{1}{8}$ $D \frac{1}{16}$ $E 0$ (LON)

Answer

The fact that it is the fourth boy tossing the coin is not relevant. The probability is the same as for any boy to toss a head, which is $\frac{1}{2}$. Answer A.

3. In an election with just two candidates, x voters voted for candidate A and 30 voted for candidate B. If a voter is to be picked at random, write down an expression for the probability that a voter will be picked who voted for candidate A. In a second election with the same two candidates, there were 30 more voters altogether, but 4 fewer voted for candidate A. If, again, a voter is to be picked at random, write down an expression for the probability that a voter will be picked who voted for candidate A. Given that the first probability is twice the second probability, form a quadratic equation in x. Hence find the value of x. (LON)

Answer The number voting for A was x, so the probability of picking an x voter is $\frac{x}{30+x}$ since the total number of voters was $30 + x$.

In the second election, the number voting for x was $x - 4$, and the total number of voters was $x + 30 + 30 = x + 60$. So the probability of an x voter is $\frac{x-4}{x+60}$.

The first is twice the second, so that

$$\frac{x}{30+x} = \frac{2(x-4)}{x+60}$$

Cross multiply

$$x(x + 60) = 2(x - 4)(x + 30)$$

Multiply out

$$x^2 + 60x = 2x^2 - 8x + 60x - 240$$

Simplify

$$x^2 - 8x - 240 = 0$$

Factorize

$$(x - 20)(x + 12) = 0$$

So $x = 20$ or $x = -12$. But since x measures the number of votes, it must be positive. The answer is $x = 20$.

4. Calculate the probability that when three fair coins are tossed they all show heads.

Answer   **Comments**

The outcomes are

HHH	HTT
HHT	THT
HTH	TTH
THH	TTT

the order is important; HHT and HTH are counted as different outcomes

There are 8 possible outcomes.
Only 1 has three heads.
The probability is $\frac{1}{8}$.

5. A die is in the shape of a cube. Its faces are numbered 1, 1, 2, 2, 3 and 4 as shown in the diagram.

number one on hidden face

Calculate the probabilities that
(i) In one throw of the die, the score is (a) 1, (b) 2, (c) 3, (d) 4.
(ii) In two successive throws, the scores are 1 and then 2.
(iii) In two successive throws, the total score is 4.
(iv) In two successive throws, the total score is even.

Answer   **Comments**

(i) (a) Two faces show a 1, and there are 6
possible faces.

$p(1)$ = probability of a 1 = $\dfrac{2}{6} = \dfrac{1}{3}$.

(b) There are also two faces with a 2, so
$p(2) = \dfrac{1}{3}$.

(c) Only one face has a 3, so $p(3) = \dfrac{1}{6}$.

(d) Similarly $p(4) = \dfrac{1}{6}$.

(ii) $p(1 \text{ then } 2) = p(1)p(2)$ independent

$\qquad = \dfrac{1}{3} \times \dfrac{1}{3} = \dfrac{1}{9}$.

(iii) A total of 4 can be obtained by 1 then 3,
2 then 2, or 3 then 1.

$p(1, 3) = p(1)p(3) = \dfrac{1}{3} \times \dfrac{1}{6} = \dfrac{1}{18}$ independent

$p(2, 2) = \dfrac{1}{3} \times \dfrac{1}{3} = \dfrac{1}{9}$

$p(3, 1) = p(3)p(1) = \dfrac{1}{6} \times \dfrac{1}{3} = \dfrac{1}{18}$

Adding, the total is $\dfrac{1}{18} + \dfrac{1}{9} + \dfrac{1}{18} = \dfrac{2}{9}$ mutually exclusive

(iv) Even total scores can be

2: 1 then 1 $p(1, 1) = \dfrac{1}{3} \times \dfrac{1}{3} = \dfrac{1}{9}$

4: with probability $\dfrac{2}{9}$ as in (iii) above

6: 3 and 3 $p(3)p(3) = \dfrac{1}{6} \times \dfrac{1}{6} = \dfrac{1}{36}$

   2 and 4 $p(2)p(4) = \dfrac{1}{3} \times \dfrac{1}{6} = \dfrac{1}{18}$

   4 and 2 $p(4)p(2) = \dfrac{1}{6} \times \dfrac{1}{3} = \dfrac{1}{18}$

8: 4 and 4 $p(4)p(4) = \dfrac{1}{6} \times \dfrac{1}{6} = \dfrac{1}{36}$

Adding, the probability of an even score is

$$\dfrac{1}{9} + \dfrac{2}{9} + \dfrac{1}{36} + \dfrac{1}{18} + \dfrac{1}{18} + \dfrac{1}{36} = \dfrac{18}{36} = \dfrac{1}{2}.$$

6. *A bag contains 6 green and 9 red counters. The counters are drawn at random, one at a time, and are not replaced. Calculate the probability that:*

(i) The first counter is green.

(ii) The first two counters are green.

(iii) At least one of the two counters is red.

(iv) If three counters are drawn, then just one of them is green.

Another bag contains 6 green and 9 red counters. Three counters are drawn in succession, each one being replaced before the next one is drawn. What is the probability that at least one of the three counters is red? (OXF)

Answer

(i) $p(G) = \dfrac{6}{6+9} = \dfrac{6}{15} = \dfrac{2}{5}$

(ii) $p(GG) = \dfrac{6}{15} \times \dfrac{5}{14}$

$\qquad = \dfrac{1}{7}$

Comments

without replacement, there are only 5 green ones left, out of 14 counters altogether

(iii) p(at least one red) $= 1 - p$(both green)

$$= 1 - \frac{1}{7} = \frac{6}{7}$$

(iv) p(one green)   write out the

$= p(RRG) + p(RGR) + p(GRR)$ possibilities

$$= \frac{9}{15} \times \frac{8}{14} \times \frac{6}{13} + \frac{9}{15} \times \frac{6}{14} \times \frac{8}{13} + \frac{6}{15} \times \frac{9}{14} \times \frac{8}{13}$$

$$= \frac{1\,296}{2\,730}$$

Now taking the case where the counters are replaced, so that the successive probabilities are not changed

p(at least one red) $= 1 - p$(all green)

$$= 1 - \frac{6}{9} \times \frac{6}{9} \times \frac{6}{9} = 1 - \frac{2}{3} \times \frac{2}{3} \times \frac{2}{3}$$

$$= 1 - \frac{8}{27} = \frac{19}{27}$$

Tree Diagrams

These are useful when several events are to happen one after the other. Each branch of the tree represents a possible outcome.

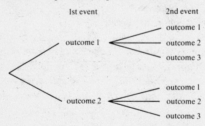

The probability of each part of the branch is written on the branch. The probability of the combined outcome represented by a whole branch is found by *multiplying* the probabilities met on the way to the end.

If a particular outcome can be arrived at by taking several routes through the tree, then the separate probabilities at the end of each branch are added to get the total probability.

Example

Each member of a class of thirty boys supports one and only one of 3 football teams; 13 boys support City, 10 support Rovers and 7 support United.

(a) If a boy is to be chosen at random, what is the probability that he will support City?

(b) If two boys are to be chosen at random, what is the probability that they will both support City?

Draw a tree diagram to show all the possible outcomes of choosing 2 boys at random, showing the probabilities of each outcome. Hence find

(c) The probability that the two boys will support the same team.

(b) The probability that the two boys chosen will support different teams. (LON)

Answer (a) The probability that he supports City $= \frac{13}{30}$ since there are 13 City supporters out of the class of 30 boys.

(b) The probability that the second boy supports City as well is $\frac{12}{29}$ since there are now only 12 City supporters and 29 boys, as the first boy has already been chosen. The probability that they both support City is found by multiplying, $\dfrac{13}{30} \times \dfrac{12}{29} = \dfrac{26}{145}$.

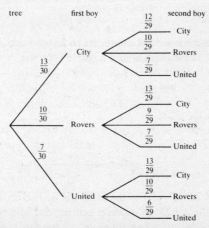

(c) The probability they support the same team = probability they support City + probability they support Rovers + probability they support United $= \frac{13}{30} \times \frac{12}{29} + \frac{10}{30} \times \frac{9}{29} + \frac{7}{30} \times \frac{6}{29}$ (from the tree) $= \frac{156}{870} + \frac{90}{870} + \frac{42}{870}$ $= \frac{288}{870} = \frac{48}{145}$.

(d) The probability they support different teams = 1 − the probability that they support the same team $= 1 - \frac{48}{145} = \frac{97}{145}$.

Using Tables and Calculators: Some General Rules

Tables

For multiplication and division problems use logarithm tables. Some books of tables have two sets of logarithms, natural logs and logs to base 10. You should always use the logs to base 10.

To look up the log of a number:

(i) Put the number in standard form (see p. 19):

$$12 \cdot 8 = 1 \cdot 28 \times 10^1$$

(ii) Look up the number part in the tables, and put the log *after* a decimal point. This is called the *mantissa*.

(iii) Take the power of 10 and place it in front of the decimal point. The power is called the *characteristic* of the log.

If the power is *negative*, then put the − sign *above* the characteristic. For example, to find the log of 0·2346:

(i) $0 \cdot 2346 = 2 \cdot 346 \times 10^{-1}$

(ii) From tables, the mantissa is found by:

　(a) Find the first two digits in the left-hand column.

　(b) Move to the column with the third digit above it; write down the entry in the table.

　(c) In the same row, move to the column headed by the fourth digit, in the *right-hand* section of the table. Add the entry here to the result of (b).

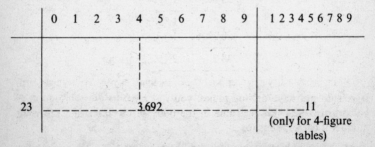

The mantissa is $3\,692 + 11 = 3\,703$.
  (iii) The characteristic is $-1 = \bar{1}$
The log of 0·2346 is $\bar{1}$·3703.

When two numbers are to be multiplied, find their logs and *add* them. The result is then looked up in *antilog tables*. The procedure for using antilog tables is very similar to that for using logs:
  (i) Look up the mantissa part of the log in the tables.
  (ii) The characteristic gives the power of 10 that the answer to (i) should be multiplied by.
When two numbers are to be divided, *subtract* the logs.
  These procedures can be written as the formulae:

$$\log(xy) = \log x + \log y$$

and
$$\log\left(\frac{x}{y}\right) = \log x - \log y$$

To raise a number to a power, look up its log, then multiply the log by the given power. Finally antilog.

$$\log(x^n) = n\log(x).$$

When using log tables for calculations, set out your working in a table.

Example Find
$$\frac{1·234 \times 54·8}{0·2346}$$

Set out as

number	log
1·234	0·0913
× 54·8	1·7388 +
	1·8301
÷ 0·2346	$\bar{1}$·3703 −
288·2	2·4598 (antilog)

If you do not have antilog tables, you will have to use the log tables backwards. Find the log value in the body of the table and see what number it corresponds to.

Squares

These tables are used in exactly the same way as log tables. The decimal point is ignored in the tables; it is up to you to decide where it should go in the answer. The best way is to write the number in standard form, and then doubling the power gives the position of the point.

Example Square $123\cdot6 = 1\cdot236 \times 10^2$ (standard form)
From table, 1 236 corresponds to 1 528. The power of 10 was 2, doubling gives 4. The answer is $1\cdot528 \times 10^4$ which can be written as 15 280.

Square roots

The tables are sometimes split up, with one for numbers between 0 and 10 and another for numbers between 10 and 100. Numbers between 100 and 1 000 are then looked up in the first table and the answer multiplied by 10. Numbers between 1 000 and 10 000 are looked up in the second table, and the answer multiplied by 100, and so on.

For numbers less than 1, write them as fractions with denominators an even power of 10, and find the square root of numerator and denominator separately.

Example $\sqrt{0\cdot0081} = \sqrt{\frac{81}{10\,000}} = \frac{9}{100} = 0\cdot09$

Sines, cosines and tangents (the tables call them *natural sines*)

If the angle is in decimals of a degree, then use the tables like logs, except that the figure in the right-hand part of the table corresponding to the fourth digit is *subtracted* in the case of cosines. If the angle is in degrees and minutes, look up in the column corresponding to the nearest number of minutes *less* than the one required, and then make up to the right figure by adding from the right-hand part of the table.

Example Find the sin of $45°\,20'$.

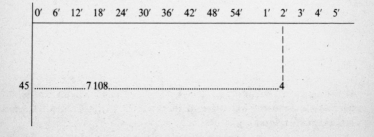

The answer is sin $45°20' = 0.7108 + 0.0004 = 0.7112$.

To find an angle with a given sin, cos or tan, find the given number in the body of the table, and see what angle it corresponds to.

Calculators

These are much easier to use. For adding, subtracting, multiplying and dividing, key in the first number followed by the correct operation key, and then the second number. Remember to press the = sign after each complete step.

You should write down the answer to each step; this makes it easier to check your working.

Square roots involve the use of the key marked with a $\sqrt{}$.

Squares can be found by keying in the number and pressing the x^2 button. On many calculators you have to press the INV key first, followed by $\sqrt{}$ key.

To find the sin, cos or tan of an angle, enter the angle in decimals and then press the appropriate sin, cos or tan key.

To find the angle corresponding to a given sin, cos or tan, enter the given number and press INV, SIN. (On some calculators you press ARC, SIN.)

The golden rule is, press the keys carefully, and write down the answer at each stage. When using sin, cos or tan, make sure that the calculator is set to *degrees*.

Technical Terms and Definitions

A acceleration   rate of change of velocity, found by differentiating: $\dfrac{\mathrm{d}v}{\mathrm{d}t}$

      acute angle   smaller than 90°

      adjacent side   joins the angle to the right angle in a triangle

      algebra   rules for using formulae and expressions

      altitude   line through a vertex of a triangle, which meets the opposite side at right angles. It gives the height of the triangle

      arc   part of circumference of a circle

      average   total of a list of numbers divided by the number of numbers

      axes   two perpendicular lines that provide the scales for drawing graphs: x-axis and y-axis

B bar chart   statistical diagram made from strips. The height of each strip is equal to the frequency

      bearing   angle that the line from a reference point to the object point makes with the North in a clockwise direction

      binary   numbers in base two, using only digits 1 and 0

      bisector   line that cuts in half. Angle bisector cuts an angle into equal halves. Perpendicular bisector cuts a line segment into equal halves, and makes a right angle with the line segment

      brackets   used to separate expressions in formulae, and for making the meaning clearer

C chord   line joining two points on a circle

      circumcircle   circle passing through the vertices of a triangle

      circumference   the edge of a circle

      coefficient   number multiplying a particular term

      common factor   divides two or more numbers or expressions

	complement	of a set is all the elements outside the set
	cone	pointed shape on a circular base
	congruent	having the same size and shape
	coordinates	numbers which specify the position of a point: $(1, 2)$ x-coordinate $= 1$, y-coordinate $= 2$
	cosine	adjacent side/hypotenuse
	cumulative frequency	frequencies added step by step
	cyclic quadrilateral	four-sided figure with vertices on the circumference of a circle
D	decagon	ten-sided figure
	decimal places	number of digits after the decimal point
	definite integral	when numbers are put into the result of integrating: $\displaystyle\int_{1}^{2} x^2 \, \mathrm{d}x$, for example
	denominator	bottom of a fraction
	depression (angle of)	angle that your line of sight makes with the object when looking down
	diagonal	line joining opposite points of a figure
	differentiation	method for calculating gradients
	domain (of a function)	set of values that you can put in
E	element	member of a set
	elevation (angle of)	angle that your line of sight makes with the object when looking up
	empty set	$\varnothing$, has nothing in it
	equation	relation satisfied by a few values of the variable; $2x - 3 = 4$, satisfied by $x = 3\cdot5$
	equilateral	equal-sided (triangle)
	event	something that happens; in probability
	expression	combination of letters and numbers
	exterior angle	outside angle

F	factor	divides a quantity exactly with no remainder
	factorizing	expressing as a product of factors
	frequency	number of occurrences of a given event
	function	rule for working out a number from the given value of the variable
G	gradient	how quickly a function or graph changes; can be found by differentiating
	graph	picture of a function
H	hemisphere	half a sphere
	hexagon	six-sided figure
	hypotenuse	longest side of a triangle
I	identity	has no effect when multiplying other elements: identity matrix $\left(\begin{smallmatrix} 1 & 0 \\ 0 & 1 \end{smallmatrix}\right)$
	index, indices (*pl.*)	another term for power (see p. 19)
	inequality	less than or greater than: $<, >$
	inscribed circle	circle touching the insides of a triangle
	integer	positive or negative whole number
	integration	opposite of differentiation; used to find areas
	interior angle	angle inside a figure
	intersection	overlap of two sets denoted by $\cap$
	inverse	opposite
	irrational	number that cannot be written as a fraction: $\sqrt{2}, \sqrt{3}$
	isosceles	triangle with two equal sides
K	kite	quadrilateral with pairs of equal sides
L	latitude and longitude	angles which give a position on the surface of the earth
	line segment	part of a line which joins two points
	linear equation	contains first power of the variable only: $y = mx + c$
	locus	path that a moving point traces out
	lowest terms	when a fraction has no factors common to top and bottom
M	mapping	rule for associating pairs of elements
	matrix	looks like $\left(\begin{smallmatrix} 1 & 4 \\ 3 & 5 \end{smallmatrix}\right)$; represents a transformation
	maximum	top of a hill on a graph

	mean	usual average of numbers
	median	middle number of a set of ordered numbers
	minimum	bottom of a valley on a graph
	mixed number	a number with, say, integer and fraction parts: $1\frac{2}{3}$
	mode	most frequent of a set of numbers
	modulo	remainder on division by a given number
	modulus	length of a vector
N	natural numbers	positive whole numbers: 1, 2, 3, . . ., and zero
	nonagon	nine-sided figure
	number line	line with the numbers marked along it
	numerator	top of a fraction
O	obtuse angle	larger than 90°
	octagon	eight-sided figure
	operation	combination rule
P	parallel	having the same direction
	parallelogram	quadrilateral with parallel sides
	pentagon	five-sided figure
	percentage	%, fraction with 100 as denominator
	perimeter	edge of a figure
	pie chart	circle divided into sectors proportional to numbers given in the data
	plane	flat surface. x–y plane, surface with points given in terms of x- and y-coordinates
	power	when a quantity is multiplied by itself a number of times: 3 with power $4 = 3 \times 3 \times 3 \times 3 = 81$
	prime numbers	have no factors apart from 1 and themselves: 2, 3, 5, 7, 11, . . .
	prism	figure with constant cross-section
	probability	the chance that an event occurs: $p(A)$
	proportionality	$y \propto x$, y increases at the same rate as x
	Pythagoras' Theorem	in a right-angled triangle it is used to calculate sides: $a^2 = b^2 + c^2$
Q	quadratic equation	x up to power 2: $ax^2 + bx + c = 0$
	quadrilateral	four-sided figure
	quartile	statistical figure: the numbers corresponding to the 25% and 75% marks on cumulative frequency axis

R	radius	line joining the centre of a circle to the circumference
	rates	local tax on property, given as p in the £
	ratio	division into given proportions: $2:3$
	rational number	fraction
	reciprocal	1 over the number
	rectangle	quadrilateral with right angles
	regular figure	has equal sides and equal angles
	rhombus	quadrilateral with equal sides
	right angle	$90°$
	right-angled triangle	has an angle of $90°$ in it
S	secant	cuts through a circle
	sector	slice of circle formed by radii
	segment	piece of a circle cut off by a chord
	sequence	list of numbers
	set	collection of elements
	significant figures	number of digits for a given accuracy
	similar	having the same shape
	simplifying	removing brackets and tidying up
	simultaneous equations	two equations in x and y, to be solved at the same time
	sine	opposite side/hypotenuse
	speed	rate of change of position: $\frac{dx}{dt}$
	sphere	ball
	square (of a number)	when the number is multiplied by itself: $x^2 = xx$
	square (shape)	rectangle with equal sides
	square root (of a number)	a quantity that gives the required number when squared: written as: $\sqrt{4} = 2$ as $2^2 = 4$
	standard form	number expressed as a number × power of ten: $a \times 10^n$ where $1 \leqslant a < 10$ and n is an integer
	subtended	the angle subtended by the two points A and B at a third point C is the angle ACB
T	tangent	line touching a curve, or opposite side/adjacent side
	transformation	rule for moving points or vectors around the plane, e.g. reflection, enlargement or rotation; represented by matrices

	trapezium	quadrilateral with only one pair of parallel sides
	tree diagram	used in probability: the possible events branch out
	triangle	three-sided figure
	trigonometry	sines, cosines and tangents
	turning point	maximum or minimum point on a curve; found by setting $\frac{dy}{dx} = 0$
U	union	combination of two sets when all their elements are put together; denoted by $\cup$
	universal set	ξ, contains all the elements for a particular problem
V	variables	the numbers put into a formula, which can have different values
	variation	same as proportionality
	vector	$\overline{AB}$, the movement from A to B; can be put in the form of a column, e.g. $\binom{1}{2}$
	Venn diagram	diagram representing sets

PENGUIN PASSNOTES

Carefully tailored to the requirements of the main examination boards (for O-level or CSE exams), Penguin Passnotes are an invaluable companion to your studies.

Covering a wide range of English Literature texts, as well as many other subjects, Penguin Passnotes will include:

ENGLISH LITERATURE

As You Like It
Henry IV, Part I
Julius Caesar
Macbeth
The Merchant of Venice
Romeo and Juliet
Twelfth Night
The Prologue to the Canterbury Tales
Cider With Rosie

Great Expectations
Jane Eyre
A Man For All Seasons
The Mayor of Casterbridge
Pride and Prejudice
Silas Marner
To Kill a Mockingbird
The Woman in White
Wuthering Heights

and OTHER AREAS

Biology
Chemistry
Economics
English Language
French
Geography

Human Biology
Mathematics
Modern Mathematics
Modern World History
Physics

PENGUIN MASTERSTUDIES

Penguin Masterstudies are written by experts to enhance literary appreciation and understanding and are suitable for literary study at advanced and undergraduate level. They are also available in other subjects.

The Penguin Masterstudies will include:

ENGLISH LITERATURE

Hamlet
Measure for Measure
Othello
The Prologue to the Canterbury Tales
The Miller's Tale

The Nun's Priest's Tale
Emma and *Persuasion*
Mill on the Floss
Vanity Fair
The Waste Land

and OTHER AREAS

Biology
Chemistry
Geography

Mathematics Vol I Pure
Mathematics Vol II Applied
Physics

A CHOICE OF PENGUINS

☐ *Man and the Natural World* **Keith Thomas** £4.95

Changing attitudes in England, 1500–1800. 'An encyclopedic study of man's relationship to animals and plants . . . a book to read again and again' – Paul Theroux, *Sunday Times* Books of the Year

☐ *Jean Rhys: Letters 1931–66*
Edited by Francis Wyndham and Diana Melly £3.95

'Eloquent and invaluable . . . her life emerges, and with it a portrait of an unexpectedly indomitable figure' – Marina Warner in the *Sunday Times*

☐ *The French Revolution* **Christopher Hibbert** £4.50

'One of the best accounts of the Revolution that I know . . . Mr Hibbert is outstanding' – J. H. Plumb in the *Sunday Telegraph*

☐ *Isak Dinesen* **Judith Thurman** £4.95

The acclaimed life of Karen Blixen, 'beautiful bride, disappointed wife, radiant lover, bereft and widowed woman, writer, sibyl, Scheherazade, child of Lucifer, Baroness; always a unique human being . . . an assiduously researched and finely narrated biography' – *Books & Bookmen*

☐ *The Amateur Naturalist*
Gerald Durrell with Lee Durrell £4.95

'Delight . . . on every page . . . packed with authoritative writing, learning without pomposity . . . it represents a real bargain' – *The Times Educational Supplement.* 'What treats are in store for the average British household' – *Daily Express*

☐ *When the Wind Blows* **Raymond Briggs** £2.95

'A visual parable against nuclear war: all the more chilling for being in the form of a strip cartoon' – *Sunday Times*. 'The most eloquent anti-Bomb statement you are likely to read' – *Daily Mail*

A CHOICE OF PENGUINS

☐ **The Complete Penguin Stereo Record and Cassette Guide**
Greenfield, Layton and March £7.95

A new edition, now including information on compact discs. 'One of the few indispensables on the record collector's bookshelf' – *Gramophone*

☐ **Selected Letters of Malcolm Lowry**
Edited by Harvey Breit and Margerie Bonner Lowry £5.95

'Lowry emerges from these letters not only as an extremely interesting man, but also a lovable one' – Philip Toynbee

☐ **The First Day on the Somme**
Martin Middlebrook £3.95

1 July 1916 was the blackest day of slaughter in the history of the British Army. 'The soldiers receive the best service a historian can provide: their story told in their own words' – *Guardian*

☐ **A Better Class of Person** John Osborne £2.50

The playwright's autobiography, 1929–56. 'Splendidly enjoyable' – John Mortimer. 'One of the best, richest and most bitterly truthful autobiographies that I have ever read' – Melvyn Bragg

☐ **The Winning Streak** Goldsmith and Clutterbuck £2.95

Marks & Spencer, Saatchi & Saatchi, United Biscuits, GEC . . . The UK's top companies reveal their formulas for success, in an important and stimulating book that no British manager can afford to ignore.

☐ **The First World War** A. J. P. Taylor £4.95

'He manages in some 200 illustrated pages to say almost everything that is important . . . A special text . . . a remarkable collection of photographs' – *Observer*